THE DOGS
WHO CAME
TO STAY

· *George Pitcher* ·

THE DOGS WHO CAME TO STAY

with drawings by TOM GEORGE

Weidenfeld & Nicolson
LONDON

First published in Great Britain in 1996 by
Weidenfeld & Nicolson

The Orion Publishing Group Ltd
Orion House
5 Upper Saint Martin's Lane
London WC2H 9EA

Second impression 1997

Originally published in 1995 by Dutton, an imprint of Dutton Signet,
a division of Penguin Books USA Inc.

Copyright © 1996 George Pitcher

'If I can stop one Heart from breaking', reprinted by permission of the
publishers and the Trustees of Amherst College from *The Poems
of Emily Dickinson*, Thomas H Johnson ed., Cambridge Mass.:
The Belknap Press of Harvard University Press, Copyright © 1951,
1955, 1979, 1983 by the President and Fellows of Harvard College.

'Or Death and December', from *Luck's Shining Child: A Miscellany
of Poems & Verses by George Garrett* (Palaemon Press, 1981), p. 11.
Reprinted by permission of the author.

George Pitcher has asserted his moral right to be identified
as the author of this work

A catalogue reference is available from the
British Library

ISBN 0 297 81850 3

Printed and bound in Great Britain by
Butler & Tanner Ltd, Frome and London

for
Nini Borgerhoff
who loved them

CONTENTS

Note: Drawings by Tom George appear on pages 11, 27, 37, 57, 81, 101, 122, and 133.

A selection of family snapshots follows page 118.

PREFACE

This is a true account, as true as I have been able to make it, of how two dogs, Lupa and Remus, entered my life, and that of my friend Ed Cone, and changed everything. It records the adventures, the joys, the sorrows, we shared with these wonderful creatures. It is the story of how they enriched our lives.

To my friend Tom George I am profoundly grateful for his sensitive drawings of the dogs. For reading drafts of the manuscript and making invaluable suggestions, I am indebted to Nini Borgerhoff, Ed Cone, Laverne and Tom George, Dick Ludwig, Victoria Newhouse, Nancy and Tom Regan, and Alan Williams. I also owe debts of thanks to Rosalie Siegel, my agent, for her constant encouragement, and to Joan Mellen, for the essential part she played in the publication of this book. I have been extremely fortunate to have William Abrahams as my editor at Dutton.

I take this opportunity to express my thanks to many friends· for their hospitality to Lupa and Remus over the years, and especially to Lucius and Jane Wilmerding, who, though they had two dogs of their own, often invited Ed Cone and me to bring our dogs along for vacations at their beautiful camp in Maine.

P_{ART} O_{NE}

I

October 1974

"Come see this!" I said to Ed from my washing-up place at the sink. We had finished lunch on this sunny mid-October day, and through the kitchen window, I watched as a medium-sized dog, obviously a female, moved warily across the backyard. She had a dull coat with the familiar black-and-tan coloration that you find in Dobermans and Rottweilers, though she belonged, I felt sure, to no recognized breed. On her wide chest she carried a large cross of white fur, as though she belonged to an order of canine nuns. Creeping close to the ground, her great pointed ears, like a bat's, stiffly alert, she looked as though she wanted, above all, not to be noticed. If she was a nun, she was a fallen one, for she was either about to have a litter of puppies or had just had them. Her long, full teats swung heavily as she went, the nipples brushing against the wet grass, too tall from heavy rains and no cutting.

"Lord, I hope she doesn't have her puppies on our property," said Ed. The voice of reason. Ed Cone was a professor of music at the university here in Princeton, and I was a professor of philosophy. We'd been sharing this handsome Victorian house on College Road, across from the theological seminary, for more than five years, two middle-aged bachelors caught up in the frantic rush of academic life—lectures to prepare, research to be done, endless meetings to attend. What's more, I was going to New York three times a week to see a psychoanalyst. So we had no extra energy, no time, to deal with a stray bitch and a litter of puppies.

"Hmm," I replied as I watched the intruder leave the yard through the open gate by the toolshed, her tail between her legs, as though she were fleeing the scene of a crime. I couldn't help being touched by this dark creature, alone in the world, with a gang of puppies to look after. And winter coming on. Somewhere inside me the subversive, irrational hope was already forming that she *would* have her puppies on our property.

We didn't see her for a few days, so we assumed she'd judged our place to be unsuitable for starting a family. But I found myself thinking about her and about the dogs I had owned in my youth. I remembered Queenie, a gentle German shepherd whom I enticed back to our house one day when I was seven years old.

"She just followed me home," I announced, all innocence.

My father, a quiet man, defeated by the Great Depression and a resident mother-in-law, smiled wearily. "Not again," he said shaking his head.

"Really, George, you must stop bringing these dogs home," said Mother, not very sternly. "You know we can't keep her."

I didn't know it, and I was bitterly disappointed, for spoiled as I was, I thought of nothing but what I wanted. And what I wanted above all was a friend. There were no boys my age in our neighborhood, so I had no pals, no playmates, and this great German shepherd, I felt instinctively, could fill that need. I didn't stop to think that I was too young to look after a dog myself, and that neither of my parents was in any condition to do so. Dad commuted from our house in New Jersey to a poor-paying job in Brooklyn (the trip took two hours each way), and Mother was on her feet all day in the rug department on the sixth floor of Bamberger's department store in Newark. They were nervous, constantly worried about money, and just plain worn out. A dog was not to be thought of.

Since Queenie wore a collar and was well trained, she

must have belonged to someone, but try as they might, my parents couldn't find the owners, so I was allowed to keep her. Poor creature, I doubt that she had much fun or got much exercise, but she was greatly loved. She slept in the cellar, where I rushed down to greet her each morning. Even now, the memory of the smell of dog, cellar, and coal burning in the furnace can revive in me the excitement I felt at owning my very first dog. One morning I found her licking four wet puppies at her side. That should be the beginning of a happy episode in my life, but strange to say, Queenie's fate, and that of her puppies, are shrouded in darkness; I simply cannot remember what happened to them. I hope I am not blocking out of my mind, as I often do, something frightful.

And later, when I was eleven or twelve, there was Joe, a beautiful English setter who had been kept tied up outside a chemical factory where Dad then worked. Joe was a wild thing. When I let him go in the field behind the school near our house, he raced in all directions, out of his mind with joy at being free, overwhelmed by all the strange new—nonchemical—smells. Only exhaustion brought him back to me and his leash.

Joe slept outdoors at night, under my bedroom window, a long metal chain allowing him access to his house and to much of the backyard. One spring, in the middle of the night, I was awakened by the sound of rattling chain, but when I looked down at the backyard, bathed in moonlight, all was quiet, so I went back to bed. In the morning, Joe was gone—someone had stolen him. Two weeks later, after I had abandoned any hope of ever seeing him again, he showed up, ten pounds lighter, covered with mud, and around his neck, a length of clothesline that he had bitten off. He slept indoors after that.

I have a snapshot of Joe and me at the Jersey shore. It is 1937 and I am twelve years old: there I am in my bathing suit, grinning, Joe standing on his hind legs with his forepaws in my hands. The top of his beautiful black-and-white head just reaches my skinny chest. It is evident that we are mad about each other.

One day the following fall when I came home from school, my mother, oddly, was not at work, but waiting for me. Joe was not there.

"A nice man came and took Joe to his farm, dear," my mother said. "He'll be much happier there—and safer—because you know how dangerous the traffic here on Gregory Avenue is for a dog like Joe."

My mind went instantly white, blank: utter incomprehension. "Can I ever go see him?" was all I could think of to say. I didn't notice my mother's reddened eyes.

"Well, dear, I don't really think that would be a very good idea. He's got to get used to ..."

But I was already rushing up to the bedroom I shared with my older brother, where I lay on my bed for hours. Were there tears, either then or later? I don't remember any, and I didn't beg for a reversal of this sudden decision from on high. It was decreed that Joe must go, and I simply accepted it. I was not torn apart by grief; on the contrary, my emotions had been relegated to the deep freeze. Like a zombie, I felt nothing. When was it—maybe a year later—that I learned what I might have known from the start: that Joe, having eaten some poison, had died that day?

Poor Mother! Her decision to protect me from knowledge of Joe's death was of course disastrously misguided. I must have hated her for what I could only regard as an act of heartless treachery. It would have been far better for me to face Joe's death—to weep for him, to be inconsolable, as I surely would have been—instead of burying my emotions. (Burying them alive, I'm tempted to say.) My mother, always overly protective of her "baby," had once again kept me from coping with the reality of death. I didn't learn to deal with it until much, much later.

A few days after our sighting of the bitch, I went into the toolshed to get a shovel, wanting to dig up some gladiolus bulbs before they froze. As I entered, I heard a sound, faint but clear, that I felt sure was the mewing of a cat, or more exactly, of a kitten. The sound stopped at once, and I began to look for the little animal. Anyone who had seen my office in 1879 Hall on the campus, or my quarters on the third floor of our house, would have known that neatness is not something I can, or anyway do, indulge in. Some of the ancients thought that God introduced order out of chaos, but I seem to function in the reverse mode. So the toolshed was then, as it is now, a jumble of flower pots, rolls of chicken wire, lengths of string and rope, bags of potting soil and bone meal and dried cow manure, watering cans, buckets, nonworking sprinklers, empty packets of seeds, unusable work gloves, stakes of various lengths, various objects without names, even a few tools. Since the shed is small—perhaps six feet by eight—a kitten could surely not remain hidden for long, despite the mess, but after fifteen minutes of lifting and shifting everything in sight, no creature was revealed.

Then it dawned on me that the sound must have come from under the shed. "That stray dog!" I thought, and my heart began to beat faster. Until three weeks ago, there had been no room for any animal of serious size to crawl under the shed. It had been built without a foundation, and the lowest boards, resting on the ground, had rotted, causing it to lean perilously southward, toward the big empty lot that sweeps gently downhill from ours. Dante Nini, a carpenter much sought after by people who value good work, had replaced the rotten boards and righted the shed by placing three concrete columns under the back, or downhill, side. Although we naturally hadn't thought of it in this light before, Dante had in fact created under the toolshed a cave that might well appeal to a wild animal looking for a winter haven.

I got a flashlight and, kneeling down behind the toolshed, I shone the light into the cave. In the darkness two luminescent blue circles confronted me and then quickly disappeared; the animal lurking there must have turned its head away from the light. Though I was sure I knew who it was, the flashlight was not bright enough for me to see her, so I rigged up our portable floodlight and again invaded her sanctuary. There she was, lying silently at the back of the cave, head averted, obviously wishing that I would go away. Not wanting to disturb her further, I shut off the light, but not before noting the barely discernible movement of tiny creatures at her side—one, two, at most three, newborn puppies. Lord, I thought, what on earth are we going to do about this?

"Guess what?" I said to Ed some time later when he came home from the university. I tried carefully as I spoke to convey the impression that something undesirable had happened. "You remember that black-and-tan dog we saw ..." He merely

The tool shed as seen from the farm, with our house beyond

groaned in response. "That's right," I went on, "she's under the toolshed. She and her puppies."

After a brief look-in at the new tenants—or squatters, really—we sat down at the kitchen table to deliberate.

"I hope you don't have any wild idea of adopting that bitch out there," Ed began.

"Well no, I—"

"Because it's quite impossible. I've got my work, and I'm just not prepared to spend hours walking a dog, taking it to the vet, and all the rest of it."

"I could do all that," I said without much conviction. I knew what was coming.

"You! You're worn out as it is, what with your compulsiveness about work and all those trips to your shrink. You even feel guilty if we go to a movie on Saturday night!"

I couldn't deny it.

"And what about our trips to Europe in the summer? You can't leave a dog in a kennel for a month every year."

I consider Ed, eight years older than I, the wisest person I know. He is, in fact, widely respected for his practical wisdom. People value his opinion and know they can count on him to express it forthrightly, not to say bluntly. So no doubt he was right in thinking that we couldn't take a dog into our already overburdened lives.

"Okay, okay," I admitted. "But look, until we think of some way to get her out of there, she'll have to be fed."

"Oh sure, she's got puppies to feed, after all. But what do you suppose she's been doing for food up until now?"

"Well, I've seen some upset garbage cans along Alexander Street. And maybe she gets handouts from the students down at the Princeton Inn."

"Yes, and I suppose she catches an occasional squirrel or rabbit." Ed shook his head. "What a life!"

So down we went to the local grocer's to buy cans of dog food and a bag of Dog Chow. We prepared a delicious dinner in an old pot and placed it at the entrance to the cave with a feeling that bordered on self-satisfaction—lords of the manor feeding the poor devils at the gates. But the expected grateful rush to our food did not happen. We were met instead with nothing but utter silence from the cave. We stepped back—ten, twenty, then thirty yards—and waited. And waited. No sign of life from within. Finally, giving up, we went back to the house. I, at least, felt let down and also, for some crazy reason, responsible for this rejection of our charitable offering.

But later, when we returned to the cave, the pot was empty and shone, in fact, as if it had just emerged, with an audible TV ad sparkle, from the dishwasher. She had accepted our food; she had eaten out of our battered old pot, so I felt that there had been a kind of interaction between her and us. I knew then that despite all the reasons against it, I wanted to get to know this wild creature.

Still, we had agreed that we couldn't possibly make room for a dog in our crowded lives, so we began to investigate ways of removing our mysterious interloper and her brood from under the toolshed, though I secretly hoped that no such way would be found. We asked Roger Breese, the police officer in charge of small animal control—what used to be called the dogcatcher—to come around and see what he could do. He looked under the toolshed and shook his head.

"Well, I suppose I could catch her with a lasso on the end of a stick and drag her out of there. Then get the puppies. But it would be a pretty rough business. There'd be a lot of thrashing around and snarling and one thing and another. She might get hurt, and of course it'd really upset her. She might even abandon her pups."

No, no, we couldn't have that.

"Well," he suggested, "if you're willing to put up with them until the puppies come out of there—in about three weeks, I reckon—I'll come back. Then it'll be much easier to round them all up."

Ed and I agreed with Breese's proposal, Ed reluctantly, and I with relief. There would be three more weeks of the excitement, anyway, I thought. I was assuming that no one would claim the dog as his own in response to the ad we had placed in *Town Topics* or to the notices we had posted at the nearby graduate college, seminary, and Princeton Inn. We did, however, receive some phone calls. One little girl, ignoring, in her despair, our careful description of the black bitch, tearfully asked if we had found her dog Mopsy, a small friendly dog with long white hair, floppy ears, and a red collar. The wife of a resident faculty advisor at the Princeton Inn called to tell us that she had often seen our bitch during the past two years, running with a pack of wild dogs. The woman had actually fed her once or twice. "Last winter," she said, "the dog slept under an overturned canoe that one of the students keeps here on the grounds of the inn. She seemed like a gentle creature, but goodness, she was shy. She never let me get close enough to touch her."

Princeton students in those days, despite the university's rule against it, often kept animals in their rooms. This meant that each June there were a dozen or so dogs and cats who had been abandoned by their not-yet-civilized masters. Visiting scholars at the Institute for Advanced Study sometimes left their temporary pets behind. In one case, a dog was abandoned in the scholar's locked apartment; by the time it was discovered, days later, it had turned savage and had to be destroyed. And

I doubt whether academic people were the only offenders. So packs of stray dogs appeared in Princeton neighborhoods and were a general nuisance. Overturned garbage cans on offal-strewn lawns and sidewalks were a common sight; joggers and children riding bicycles had been attacked. And life was desperately hard for the animals themselves. Only the tough ones, who either had innate street smarts or quickly acquired them, could survive the New Jersey winter with its freezing winds, its snowstorms—its traffic!—its short supply of food and shelter. Thinking of these things, I had to admire the gutsiness of the dingy animal who had taken refuge under our toolshed.

For two or three days, Ed and I continued to put food at the entrance to the cave, but this was an unrewarding process, for she steadfastly refused to show even so much as the tip of her nose, no matter how long we stood there waiting for her to emerge. Indeed, we scarcely ever saw her at all. If she happened to be outside the cave when one of us appeared near the toolshed, she would immediately run off, tail between her legs, to watch us from a safe distance. To be sure, this tactic of hers was preferable to some of the readily imagined alternatives. She might, for instance, have bared her teeth and driven us away from her precious brood. But still we wanted to see her close up; in particular, we wanted to see her actually eating our delectable fare.

On the advice of a visiting friend, we began putting the pot of food farther and farther away from the mouth of the cave, closer and closer to the house. One day, after about a week, the pot sat a few feet from the shed, in plain view from our kitchen windows. After waiting for what seemed a very long time, we saw her wolflike head appear around the corner of the shed. She looked carefully about the backyard, and having assured herself that no enemies were lurking, crept toward the food. But when she caught sight of us looking at her through the window, she immediately ran back to her lair without touching her dinner. I thought then, "Oh well, we have a wild animal on our hands; if I had any half-formed ideas of keeping her as a pet, I can forget them." We gave her a few minutes to come back, but when she didn't, we left the kitchen like two guilty boys. A half hour later, there in the backyard stood the empty pot.

The same little drama took place the next day, except now, after her first retreat, she poked her head around the side of the shed. She then made several cautious approaches to the food, but each time the sight of us in the kitchen sent her scurrying away—though we were trying our best to be invisible, leaping away from the window whenever she looked as if she might turn her head in our direction. In a few days, however, she was allowing us to watch her eat as long as we were inside the house; any attempt to approach her, or even to gaze at her, motionlessly, from anywhere outside the house, caused alarmed flight.

Early in November, Ed went off for three weeks to lecture in England, giving me time to sort out my thoughts about the dogs. The question hadn't come up yet, but did I want to take on one of the puppies? Well, yes, I supposed I did, but I also doubted whether my desire would be strong enough or sensible enough to withstand Ed's inevitable opposition to the idea. But that issue, I thought, could wait until we had seen the puppies and Ed was back from England. What about the mother? There seemed, on the face of it, to be no possibility of adopting her. As one of our neighbors said, "You'll never tame her. Once a wild animal, always a wild animal."

While I half agreed with this assessment, I also felt a vague but growing attraction to our mysterious guest. I didn't want to give up on her—not without making some further efforts. So, unmindful for the most part of the undesirable consequences that success would no doubt bring, I set about trying to get literally closer to her. I would try to touch her, maybe even pet her.

I continued my frequent visits to the cave; I would kneel at the entrance and speak gently into the darkness, hoping that she would sense the goodwill that lay behind my mellifluous tone of voice. But it was impossible to tell whether this practice was meeting with anything but indifference. I had to try something a bit more aggressive. A day or two after Ed's departure, as the stray was finishing her meal in the backyard—when I thought she might be most receptive to my overtures—I crept quietly outside, large dog biscuit in hand, to the back corner of the house, the corner away from the toolshed, so as to leave her escape route free. I then tried to manifest myself to her as if I weren't really there—diaphanously, so to speak. To appear as small as possible, I squatted, and held out the biscuit.

At the sight of me, she fled, just as I expected. I waited in vain for her to come back for another look. I kept trying, however, and a few days later when I once again appeared in the same spot, to my delight she retreated only as far as the side of the toolshed, where she turned and stared apprehensively at me. With her head down, her black glistening eyes fixed on me, she was the picture of mistrust. Still, she consented to remain in the same open area with me. That was progress, surely. I suddenly remembered that I had read somewhere that staring at an animal is an act of aggression, a sign that one might attack, so I looked down at the ground, only occasionally glancing up at her. Smiling, but trying not to show too many ferocious-looking teeth, I spoke to her in the gentlest voice I could summon: "Look what I have for you: a delicious doggy biscuit. Come on, now, I'm not going to hurt you. You sweet girl, just come and take it, don't be afraid. . . ."

It was clear that she was tempted by the biscuit but that she simply could not bring herself to approach a human being. (What had she endured? How must she have been mistreated!) Each of these sessions, in which I tried to appear harmless and to be irresistibly charming, ended in the same way: after ten or fifteen minutes of weighing my blandishments, she turned and crept back to her lair.

Feeling rejected and strangely hurt, and sensing at the same time a huge vulnerability in her, I was more determined than ever to get close to her. I knew that her fear of people was altogether general, but I couldn't help taking it personally: I was the one, after all, from whom she was actively keeping her distance. I wanted to show her that though her poor opinion of mankind was no doubt warranted, I, at least, meant her no harm.

Days passed with no thaw in her massive distrust of me. Whenever teaching duties, visits to my shrink, and the ordinary chores of life left me a few spare minutes, I visited the cave, hoping for an opportunity to demonstrate my goodwill. But she would lie motionless and silent, out of sight, or if I should happen to surprise her outside the cave, she would instantly run off to a safe distance.

I was sure that if it weren't for the food I set out for her, she wouldn't care whether I lived or died. Apart from the food, I was simply a nuisance, forever coming around, peering in, bothering her. She must have felt like the two potted plants in the *New Yorker* cartoon several years ago: as a glowing middle-aged woman, watering can in gloved hand, approached them, one plant said to the other, "Here we go again, yackity, yackity, yackity!"

One afternoon, when I looked into the cave, I found her, for the first time, not hidden away in utter darkness but crouching only a foot or two from where I knelt.

"Well, hello there," I said quietly, trying oh so hard not to frighten her. I scarcely dared to breathe. I wanted to reach out and touch her, but I couldn't risk it. She turned her head away, and I thought she would creep to the back of the cave, but no, she held her ground. In a moment, she began to wag her tail ever so slowly. It thumped against the side of the cave. With that gentle motion, all my defenses were instantly swept away. "Well then," I said to myself as she suddenly looked blurred to me, "I'm yours forever!"

2

New Life

The cave under the toolshed issues onto the empty lot next to ours; it is a splendid two- or three-acre parcel of land, with old trees and open spaces, that once belonged to Professor Henry Norris Russell, a distinguished Princeton astronomer of an earlier day. His Victorian house of painted brick, with a wide covered porch running almost all the way around it, was ugly but grand. It was torn down after the university bought the property from Russell's estate in 1969. I have permission from the university to grow vegetables on a part of this land, and so Ed and I call it the farm.

From my third-story window, facing south, I can see the toolshed and out over the entire farm. One perfect morning in early November while Ed was still in England, I looked down to see our stray lying contentedly in the sun, a few feet from the mouth of the cave. I'd never seen her like that before—but wait—what was this? Yes, yes, the puppies were out there with her! I raced down to greet them. Their mother, of course, immediately ran off, circling me watchfully. Instead of the two or three pups we had expected, I was astonished, no, flabbergasted, when I counted seven of them!

Five puppies had the same black-and-tan pattern as their dam, creating the illusion that here we had a genuine breed of dog. But this illusion was dispelled by the other two, who were basically white, splashed here and there with black or tan spots. There could have been two fathers of this litter: one with the same markings as the bitch, one all or mostly white. Unlike their mother, these tiny creatures had no fear of me whatsoever; they went on biting each other, running at nothing, making dubious sounds, falling down, peeing, testing everything, just as if I weren't there. The back of a dark cave was all they had known up to now; suddenly there was all *this* to explore.

One of the black-and-tans was larger than the others, and two were definite runts. My inexpert examination resulted in the uncertain but later corroborated finding that all the pups except for one black-and-tan were males. One of the runts was rather passive, somewhat intimidated by his littermates. The other runt, however, was cocky and independent; it was impossible not to pay special attention to him. He was biting sticks, picking up scraps of paper, charging at things, and though small, he took no guff from any of his larger mates. He soon came over to me, pounced on my shoelaces, and began chewing them. I squatted down to pick him up, but as I reached out for him, he put his front paws on my knee, cocked his head, and looked me straight in the eye. A look of honest inquiry, totally without fear: "Hello, what on earth are you?" he seemed to say. In a flash, I knew that I had to have this tiny creature. No thought of Ed's objections, no thoughts about the difficulties, the problems, the impossibility of it all. Only the knowledge that I had been chosen.

Afterward, I started thinking about this litter of animals. Of course they were cute, adorable, cuddly; how could a gang of three-week-old puppies be anything else? But I found it surprising not only that these little animals seemed perfectly healthy but that they were altogether as playful as puppies are supposed to be. How could such gorgeous babies come from a mother who had been feeding mostly on garbage from the moment of conception? And how could they be full of fun when their dam was frightened and depressed? I thought she must have supernatural powers; in some mysterious way she had been able to create and sustain, with almost nothing, these perfect creatures.

And then I wondered why the puppies were completely unafraid of me. How did they know I wouldn't gobble them up? Why shouldn't they be frightened by *any* animal that was forty or fifty times their size, as I was? Surely they would have behaved differently if a lion, say, had walked up to them. Science, I vaguely supposed, would say that it had to do with genes. The dog has been a domesticated species for untold centuries, and by now puppies come out of the womb knowing that a human being is, generally speaking, okay but that other large creatures—lions, for example—are not. But I didn't want to accept that story; I preferred to think that their mother, by her behavior or by some other secret signal, had told them that I was not to be feared.

I wrote to Ed with the stunning news that no less than seven puppies had emerged from the cave under our toolshed. As a note of warning, I told him that they were "dangerously cute." When he got back from England a few days later, he was as smitten by them as I was. It was difficult to resist the temptation to abandon one's work altogether and become a full-time puppy-watcher. Who could fail to be delighted, to be moved by them as they ran and played and mock-fought and stumbled and poked their noses into everything? We laughed when the cocky runt took it into his head that his mother's tail was a perfectly wonderful toy; he tried to pounce on it as she swished it for him when she was lying down, and when she'd had enough of that and got up, that was even more fun because then he could chase after her, leaping at the retreating tail with fierce little barks.

If we were very far away, the mother let us watch her suckle the pups. She seemed to go into a kind of trance as they jammed their snouts up hard into her belly or actually squeezed the milk out of her teats with their paws. In one of those You and Your Dog books we had borrowed it said that puppies should be given solid food about this time, so we laid in a supply of Puppy Chow and milk. This was a big hit with the youngsters: they mobbed us when we arrived with two dishes of food, squealing and whining in anticipation, their tails in frantic motion, their paws making a mess of our trousers. The dishes would scarcely have reached the ground when the pups would start munching and lapping, at the same time forming themselves, as if on command, into two eager circles around the dishes. After these meals, we often played with the pups, rolling them over, letting them gnaw playfully on our fingers. Their great taut tummies, their soft fur, the quick padded kicks of

Breakfast at Café Lupa

their back feet on my wrist—these things never failed to stir in me something very like paternal feelings.

Since the puppies were such a constant delight to both Ed and me, Roger Breese's earlier suggestion that he now be summoned to collect them and their mother was completely forgotten. But Ed was still adamantly against keeping any of the dogs permanently. When the puppies were eight weeks old, old enough to leave their mother, off they would all go to Jeanne Graves, director of the Small Animal Rescue League. She would find good homes for them. Overtly I had to go along with this plan, since it seemed to be the only reasonable one, but in my heart, I was fiercely rebellious. I was determined to keep the brazen runt, and ever since his mother had taken me over with the wagging of her tail, I could not think of letting her go.

I tried to find a way of countering Ed's arguments, with no success. His reasons, it seemed, couldn't be overturned because they were just too good. We really didn't have time in our hectic schedules to look after any pets. And his stand in this matter carried additional weight because he was the owner of the house we shared. Although he never alluded to this fact, I felt that if he didn't want to have dogs, then that was pretty much that.

How, then, was I to bring Ed around to my unreasonable attitude about the dogs? Clearly what I had to work on was not his mind but his heart. Should I start by getting him to confess how adorable he thought the puppies were? No, because puppies are well known for quickly turning into dogs, and we could have no idea what sort of dogs these enchanting creatures would grow up to be. So it was not the puppies but the mother who would have to bring about a change in Ed's feelings, and I soon saw what magical potion I must pour into his ear to secure this result.

"Look," I said one night over dinner, trying my best to sound offhand about it, "what do you suppose will happen to the bitch once the puppies are weaned?"

"Well," he replied, "I suppose she'll go back to her old life."

"Running around with the other wild dogs? That's a pretty rough fate, isn't it, especially in the cold weather?" Then, after a pause, as if for reflection, I added, "Of course Jeanne Graves might find a home for her."

From the way his shoulders sank and from the way he gazed out the window, I knew I'd scored a point. We both knew that not even Jeanne Graves, a genius at placing dogs of all kinds and nonkinds, would be able to find a home for the mother of our pups. For she was not very attractive: her legs were too short, her body too wide, her coat too dull.

Worse, she was inordinately shy and seemed also to be depressed, joyless.

"Who would want her?" Ed said very quietly. I knew from the pained look on his face that the hard edges of his opposition were crumbling.

Not wishing to move too quickly, I let a couple of days pass before making my next move.

"Look," I said to Ed, as if the idea had just occurred to me, "what about keeping her as an outside dog? She wouldn't be any trouble—it would just be a matter of feeding her." My thought was that this arrangement would be only a minimal change from what we had on our hands already; it would be halfway between really adopting her and not adopting her at all.

"Well," he replied with a sigh, "that's a possibility. Let's think about it."

I knew from this response that the battle was all but won; it would be merely a matter of time before he capitulated. In the days that followed, he remarked what a good mother the bitch was, gentle but firm with her charges. Lovingly, she licked their ears. She let them playfully gnaw on parts of her body until their needlelike teeth began to hurt her; then she stopped them instantly with a movement of her head and a mock growl of disapproval. She licked their bottoms to stimulate their bowel movements.

Sure enough, Ed soon acknowledged that although he hated the idea, we had no choice but to keep the stray or, at any rate, try to keep her—outside.

"What else can we do?" he said. "We can't just let her fend for herself, especially now with the cold weather coming on."

"That's right, we're stuck with her," I replied in an effort to conceal the eagerness with which I accepted our new responsibility.

"But she's not going to be what you might call a barrel of laughs exactly," he said forlornly.

"No," I agreed. "In fact, something of a drag, I suppose."

Ah this, surely, was the time to make my pitch for the feisty runt! "So why don't we adopt one of the puppies, too?" I went on. "Two dogs won't be any more trouble than one, and we might as well get some fun out of this deal."

Ed closed his eyes and, with a resigned smile, nodded his head. "You're determined to keep that little runt, aren't you! Well, all right, all right."

And so it was done. For better or worse, we had adopted two dogs.

We began thinking about names for our new charges. Since I suffer from a bad case of what my late friend and colleague

Walter Kaufmann called "decidophobia"—fear of making decisions—no name that came up seemed quite right to me. Ed eventually made the good point that the bitch, with her large stiff ears and full dugs, looked very like the wolf that suckled Romulus and Remus, and when we saw her astride the pups nursing underneath her, we were reminded of the famous statue of that Roman wolf. But what was she called? We found no answer in the books we consulted, and our friends in classics didn't know, so we settled on the Italian noun for female wolf, "Lupa." Our pup, then, had to be christened "Remus," since that name clearly fit our small, lean, confident animal better than "Romulus" did. To us the name "Romulus" for some reason suggested obesity or, at any rate, a certain roundness of shape and dimness of intelligence. No, the name "Remus" was far more suitable.

Though we never said so, we knew that giving names to the animals was a significant act: it was an acknowledgment that they were, for us anyway, something like persons, and persons, moreover, who were now our responsibility. We were committing ourselves in a serious way, as one does in taking vows.

One afternoon in early December, with winter coming fast, a freezing rain began to fall. Through the night it gathered strength until we were assailed with a storm of biblical proportions. The wind-driven water smashed down, rattling our windows. Shutters banged. Between periods of sleep, I could imagine streams forming here and there in the yard, carrying topsoil down the slope to the farm. In the morning there would be gallons of water in the cellar. But what, I kept wondering, can be happening to Lupa and her youngsters under the toolshed? Their cave would have been transformed into a muddy bog. I imagined them shivering, freezing, whimpering, maybe half crazy with fear.

At the first light of day, I got up to discover that the rain, at least, had stopped. Ed was awake, complaining that he hadn't slept well.

"Me, too," I said. "Was it the storm or the dogs?"

"Well . . . ," he answered with an I-give-up gesture of his hands, confessing that it was concern for the dogs that had kept him awake.

On our way down to the toolshed, I had to fight off images of half-drowned, ratlike creatures with glazed eyes stumbling about or maybe even too weak to move. What we saw were seven wet, muddy puppies gloriously investigating the new day, friskiness undimmed, watched over by their miraculously bone-dry mother.

As we prepared our celebratory breakfast, we saw Lupa nursing all seven of the pups. She stood by the toolshed, quietly panting, legs slightly apart to provide easier access, while the pups danced and tumbled under her, sucking out the delicious milk. As they jockeyed about for new, possibly milkier positions, she leaned over to lick an ear here, a flank there. A display of motherly affection? No doubt, but as we discovered after breakfast, it was motherly concern for cleanliness, too, for by then she had licked away every trace of mud from the puppies' coats.

Although the storm had produced no disasters, we were determined that the dogs should not spend another such night: they must move one floor up, into the toolshed itself. Into the *piano nobile.* That afternoon we cleared out a corner of the shed and put down some pieces of burlap and an old blanket, creating what we regarded as an irresistibly cozy nest. We left the door of the shed invitingly open, but none of our crew seemed to notice. There was no chance of luring Lupa into the new quarters, so we carried the puppies there one by one. One by one they scrambled away the instant they were put down, back to their familiar den below.

That night after supper, we took a flashlight and went out to the backyard to have a look. Not a puppy to be seen, but there in the corner of the toolshed, lying on the old blanket, was Lupa! She turned her head away from the light.

"Look," said Ed, "this is not a vicious dog."

(Well, no, I thought, almost offended; of course she isn't.) Kneeling down, we reached out and for the first time actually touched her. We petted her, softly spoke sweet nothings to her: "What a good girl," "Do you like that?" and such things. She lay still, head averted, as though merely putting up with this foolishness. But when, after a time, we stopped, she turned to look at us—invitingly, as it seemed to me—so I stroked her head again, and she stretched it up firmly against my hand in a gesture of unalloyed pleasure. It was something, clearly, she had longed for. And so had I.

We stayed there a long time, not saying much, content merely to be close to this wild creature who now, we felt, had at last given us a measure of trust.

The next day around dinnertime, we went out to check up on things and found Lupa again on her bed but surrounded now by her seven pups. The previous night, she had tested the place and liked it, so she had moved her family upstairs, up from the cave. But how, I wondered, had she worked this magic? The night before, the puppies understood—how?—that they were to stay below and not follow their mother, but this time they knew—again, how?—that they were to follow her up to their new quarters. Although I knew that this sort of nonlinguistic communication is quite common in the animal world, I couldn't help thinking of it as yet another of Lupa's magical powers.

Lupa and Remus were to be outdoor dogs, though, as I secretly hoped, only for a while. So now that the dogs were living in the shed, it was time to build a higher fence around the backyard than the low wire one we had inherited. Lupa was forever climbing over one of the gates, running the risk of hurting her soft belly, her low-hanging dugs. To protect her, we had tied an old bath mat on top of the gate. Her purpose, we discovered, was to find extra food, which she did with great efficiency by raiding our neighbors' garbage cans and by catching squirrels and rabbits. One day, with mixed feelings, we watched her return from one of her expeditions with a fresh rabbit haunch in her mouth. She casually tossed it to her puppies who, with as much ferocity as they were capable of, quickly devoured it. We were embarrassed, too, when Anne Poole, living directly behind us, gently informed us that her pretty formal garden seemed to be Lupa's favorite toilet. No, a higher fence was required, so Dante Nini was commissioned to erect a six-foot wooden enclosure around the backyard.

Since Dante had created the cave into which Lupa crept to have her litter, we considered him to be a kind of godfather to the puppies, and so thought it only right that he should be

· Remus at about five weeks old ·

offered one of them—whichever one he wanted, as long as it wasn't Remus. He accepted the offer and immediately chose the largest puppy, a splendid black-and-tan male whom he eventually named Chipper. Margaret Wilson, a colleague of mine in the philosophy department, and her husband Emmett, came by one day and said they'd like to adopt one of the white pups. They were to call him Norman.

Dante had several other more important projects going on while he was building our fence, so its construction took two or three weeks. Early on, Dante of course had to dig several large postholes; one day, after a heavy night rain had filled the holes with water to ground level, we were horrified to see one of the white puppies fall headfirst into a posthole, his back legs pumping wildly in the air. We quickly pulled him out, and we could laugh at his comical expression, but it was a near miss. He certainly would have drowned if we hadn't been there on the spot. The holes, need I say, were immediately covered.

One day, while the puppies were resting in the toolshed, a magnificent black-and-tan male, twice the size of Lupa, sprang easily over one of the gates and, with tail wagging, touched his nose to hers in greeting. I felt, as I watched her response, friendly but restrained, that these two dogs knew each other well. He investigated our backyard with some thoroughness, and

Lupa had no objections, but when he stuck his nose inquisitively into the toolshed, she rushed at him with hostile sounds, driving him over the gate and away. It somehow seemed obvious to me that he was the father of the five black-and-tan puppies, and so we dubbed him Big Daddy. We used to see him, always alone, wandering about town, healthy and confident, a living argument for the virtues of the unattached life. He never came back to our place. So Lupa was yet another single parent with dependent children!

As near as we could tell, the puppies would be eight weeks old in mid-December, time for them to be taken from their mother. Remus, of course, was going to stay with us, and we agreed to keep Chipper and Norman for a few extra days until the Nini and Wilson households were ready to receive their untrained puppies. We arranged for Roger Breese to take the other four pups to the animal shelter on December 15th. Jeanne Graves assured us that with Christmas coming, she would have no trouble placing them.

Breese arrived at the appointed hour, and when he turned the corner into the backyard, Lupa at once took off for the deepest reaches of the farm. Was she just running from a stranger, or did she know Breese from her earlier life? In any case, she knew what was about to happen. She knew.

Lupa's absence, though it bothered me, at least made it easier for us to round up her four unsuspecting children. All went well until the truck bearing the four puzzled youngsters disappeared out our driveway. We turned back toward the house and without warning, I started to weep. Yes, foolish, yes, quite irrational—I knew it even as the tears flowed. But I couldn't fight the thought that it was cruel for those young animals to be swept away in an instant from their mother, from their world, to an alien place of bricks and cages and strangers. Nor could I deny my sense of guilt. Ed and I had betrayed the four puppies and, above all, Lupa. Would she now continue to trust us? When she returned later and poked about everywhere for her missing pups—did I hear her whimpering?—she looked at us accusingly. I would have sworn she did.

One Sunday morning, with the new fence still not completed, we woke to find an empty backyard. Lupa's absence wasn't at all surprising, for she still went off on her foraging jaunts, but none of the puppies had ever left the compound. We looked in the toolshed, in their old cave under the shed, all around the house. They had all vanished. I was quite breathless with shock, and to make matters worse, Dante was to pick up Chipper that very afternoon.

Lurid pictures of what had happened immediately beset

me: Lupa, fed up with semicaptivity, had returned to the wild, and the three puppies had followed her. All four were now lying dead on Alexander Street, run over by cars. Poisoned meat had been thrown into the backyard, and the dogs had staggered off to die. Thieves had raided the place during the night and were going to sell the dogs to laboratories where painful experiments would be performed on them.

We searched the neighborhood, all over the nearby Springdale Golf Course and the graduate college; we went to the seminary, then to the university campus, down to the Princeton Inn. I took a quick apprehensive look at Alexander Street and found it, thank God, corpseless. Late in the morning, as we were returning home along College Road from yet another fruitless search, down from the seminary grounds pranced a happy band, Lupa in the lead, her three charges trying gamely to keep up with her. They had had a grand Sunday morning outing and were delighted with themselves. Later we found the hole under Lupa's bath-matted gate that the puppies had dug: they had been determined not to be left behind *this* time when Mum went off on one of her expeditions.

"You know," I said to Ed later during our much-delayed breakfast, "you were pretty upset when the dogs were missing. As much as I was."

"Yes, I guess I was," he answered, pouring himself a second cup of tea. Then, after a few sips, he put down his cup. "And you want to know something else?—I was moved almost to tears when I saw them running down toward us from the seminary."

In the afternoon, Dante picked up Chipper, and later that week completed his work on our new fence. We had Norman for a while after that, but then he, too, went off to his new home. We were sorry to lose him. He was devoted to Remus, and it was touching to see them sleeping next to each other, with Norman's head resting on Remus's back or his paw draped affectionately over his side.

One day at lunchtime, not long after our new life with just Lupa and Remus had begun, I called Ed excitedly to the kitchen window. Lupa was playing with one of the plastic bones we'd bought for the puppies. With a great twist of her whole body, she sent it flying, pouncing on it when it came down. With her rump in the air, she gnawed on it briefly, then shook it. Her tail high, she ran with it, she pranced, she fairly danced. Happy! Oh yes, happy!

3

$\mathcal{S}ettling \ \mathcal{I}n$

$\mathcal{T}$he animal shelter that Jeanne Graves supervised with such expert and loving care is a small, neat building off Route 206, two or three miles from the town center. Ed and I went there nearly every other day to see how our four orphaned puppies were getting on. They were split up into two pairs in adjacent cages. We usually found them lying at the back of their cages, looking rather forlorn, we thought, but when they saw us, they rushed forward with little squeals of delight to lick our hands and be petted. My impulse was to gather them up instantly and take them home.

"Those pups had a very good mother," Jeanne told us, "and two very good godfathers." I was grateful for her praise but couldn't help wondering if a really good godfather would have abandoned his godchildren in this way.

One by one, the three males were adopted, but no one seemed to want the single female of the litter. Ed and I decided after long, sometimes anguished, discussion, that we would take her if she were still unclaimed after Christmas. It's true we didn't have space for three dogs, but we thought—and I greatly feared—that Lupa might abandon us after a time. But one day, when the female, now entirely alone in the world, had become despondent, Jeanne gave her a toy bone. The puppy happened to be playing with it, tossing it up in the air and then pouncing on it (just as Lupa had done), when a man came into the shelter looking for a Christmas present for his children. Utterly charmed by her, he adopted her at once.

Now what about Lupa? We had given her a handsome bright red collar and attached tags that said she belonged to us, but did she agree with this? Was she really going to settle in quietly with us or was she just waiting for a chance to rejoin her old gang? For as long as I can remember, it has been my invariable practice to expect the worst, so in the face of growing evidence that Lupa was reasonably content with her state of domesticity, I nevertheless felt sure that she would soon answer the call of the wild.

Despite my fears, I had to agree that we could not keep

Lupa and Remus confined forever behind Dante's high wooden fence. They would have to be allowed to run and play. One bright day in December after Chipper and Norman had left, we decided it was time to allow Lupa to choose her destiny.

With her new leash in my hand, I tried my best to look jolly or, at any rate, not apprehensive as I approached Lupa. We had foolishly bought a heavy chain of huge metal links, strong enough to restrain an enraged ox. I breathed a sigh of relief when she accepted it like a lamb and allowed me to lead her about without the slightest objection. Ed hooked Remus up to a thin, puppy-weight leash, and we set off on Our First Walk. Our house is a stone's throw from the Springdale Golf Course, a lovely parklike tract perfect for walking dogs. So out we went onto the course, deserted now in mid-winter.

Keeping the dogs on the leash, we walked over toward the graduate college, following the first two holes. There was no snow on the ground, so we wouldn't be able to follow Lupa's tracks when she made her dash to freedom.

"Maybe we shouldn't release her today," I said. "Wouldn't it be better to give her some time to get used to us?"

"Come on, we've talked this all over and made our decision," replied Ed. "Let's just do it and see what happens."

So we unhooked Lupa from her leash. She looked up at us—was it to say, "Thanks, nice knowing you?"—and then dashed straight down the third fairway, full speed, toward the fourth hole and the woods beyond. We walked, not hopefully, after her, I quickly surged ahead in a trot, while Ed was forced to come at a slower pace set by Remus. I could see Lupa at the edge of the wood, nose to the ground, excitedly following the scent of rabbit, deer, who knows what. We did not exist for her.

Then she disappeared into the woods. We called, we whistled, we looked, we listened. I plunged deep into the woods, shouting her name, while Ed waited with Remus on the fringe. Nothing. When it seemed pointless to go on, we headed for home.

"Look," said Ed, putting a comforting hand on my shoulder, "she'll get tired and find her way back to our place on her own."

"Oh sure," I answered. I was certain we'd never see her again, and I could tell from Ed's expression that he felt the same way.

We kept looking back toward the woods as we went. When we got near the Princeton Inn, almost home, I turned to give one last look—and there she was! Fifty yards behind us, following slowly. As I ran toward her, she stopped. Her chest was heaving, and drops of saliva fell from the delicate tip of her heavy pink tongue. Her lips were drawn back from her slightly open jaws so that she seemed to be smiling. I saw for the first time that she was beautiful. She looked up at me as if to say, "Boy, that was great fun!" but what I understood was that she was ours, now and forever.

Lupa submitted gladly to the leash. She even accepted my bear hug and the kiss I planted on the bridge of her nose. I don't think she had any idea what all the fuss was about. But Remus now decided that he had had quite enough. He flopped down with a finality that announced that he would under no circumstances take another step. So back home we went, Lupa padding along at my side, and Remus, exhausted, happy in Ed's arms.

An early order of business was to arrange physical examinations for the two dogs. We chose Jack Blumenthal, a big, soft-spoken man in his late fifties, to be our vet, not only because he was an old friend but also because he was well known for his wonderfully gentle way with animals. Given her massive distrust of people, we weren't at all sure how Lupa would behave at her first visit to the vet. But Jack calmed us all down by talking quietly about this and that—probably about art or French food, two of his passions—while gently patting Lupa. Even when we lifted her up on the stainless steel examining table, she showed no fear, no aggression: her great ears erect, she was obviously wary, but she stood there quietly, unmoving, stoically resigned to accept whatever fate might have in store for her.

Jack judged that Lupa was probably about three years old and that she was in remarkably good shape. She was, however, infested with every worm known to medicine—except, thank God, heartworm. (The heartworm is a dreadful creature. Its eggs, deposited in a dog's blood system by an infected mosquito, hatch into long thin white worms that migrate to the heart, clogging it and eventually killing the animal.) Jack started Lupa on a regimen of pills designed to eject the unwanted tenants of her digestive tract one by one. It wasn't until nearly a year later that she could call her intestines her own.

As soon as Jack said it was okay for Lupa to be spayed— not sprayed or splayed or spaded, terms I have heard people use—we had it done. Jack's surgeon reported that Lupa had a well-used uterus; this confirmed our suspicion that Lupa had had a colorful past life, for we had begun to notice a few mid-sized black-and-tan dogs around town, some looking suspiciously like Remus or like Lupa herself. Since there is an enormous over-population of cats and dogs, many millions of unwanted animals being put to death each year, Ed and I considered it a moral duty to have Lupa spayed, but male chauvinism or—much more likely—neurotic fear of castration kept us from even entertaining the idea of having Remus altered.

The thought of Remus without his testicles would have struck me as quite horrible. If we had actually discussed the issue, I would probably have argued that to castrate Remus would be an act of mutilation and that it would change his personality, his very essence, in a terrible way, turning him into a docile, far less interesting animal. But then shouldn't I have had the same reservations about spaying Lupa? Yes, I must now humbly confess.

The plan, remember, was that Lupa and Remus were to be "outdoor dogs"; that, at least, was what Ed firmly intended. But I had it in mind that they should be outdoor dogs only until Ed relented and let them move into the house.

We built a structure of thick plywood, heavily insulated with layers of newspapers covered with canvas, in a corner of the toolshed, forming a snug house-within-a-house for them. I even insisted that we install a small electric heater on a shelf in the shed, to be turned on during the coldest winter nights.

With no great fanfare, Ed soon quietly conceded that it was ridiculous to forbid the dogs all entry into our house. He now shared my thought that there was no point in keeping the dogs if they were forever to be outside. So one day, not knowing what to expect, we let them in. Remus, of course, had never seen the inside of a house; he excitedly investigated everything—chairs, table legs, wastepaper baskets, lamps, rugs. It was a great adventure for him. We didn't know whether or not Lupa had ever been inside a house before. She crept around on full alert as if she had been parachuted into enemy territory, sniffing everywhere for danger. She thoroughly inspected the kitchen, then one room after another until she had satisfied herself that the house was, for the moment, free of hostile agents.

It turned out that Lupa was completely housebroken, so human dwellings must have figured in her past. She also taught Remus—we certainly didn't—that no self-respecting dog will answer the call of nature inside a human's house. And he was a quick learner; he peed only once, on the living-room rug. Well, he peed another time, too, but the second lapse was not his fault but ours, since he had signalled to us his desire to go out by sitting next to the back door.

This was our first encounter with what turned out to be Remus's main method of manifesting his wants, the method of "significant sitting." For example, if he wanted a dog biscuit, he simply sat near the box of biscuits and silently stared at one or the other of us. If he not merely wanted a biscuit but felt it was positively his right to have one, the silent stare was accompanied by a lowering of the head and a frown that accused us of rankest cruelty, perhaps even of criminality. This method, I may say, was highly effective. It was also original with Remus; at any rate he didn't learn it from Lupa, who did things quite differently. She told us she wanted something by placing her paw gently on our knee and looking expectantly into our eyes, perhaps also whining softly. This method, too, got results.

Although the dogs soon settled nicely into the house during the day, we continued to put them out at night to sleep in their toolshed abode. But early each morning, long before we or the neighbors wanted to start a new day, they came to the back door and barked noisily to be let in. (Since the methods of significant sitting and of paw-on-the-knee were obviously inapplicable in this case, cruder methods had to be employed.) One of our dog books—we now had a considerable collection of them—said that the best way to correct this form of behavior is to throw empty tin cans near the offending creature when it begins making the undesired racket. So we began collecting empty tin and aluminum cans. When we decided that we had collected enough of them to administer an effective lesson, I set my alarm for six the next morning.

"Ed," I said after knocking on his bedroom door, "get up, it's six o'clock. Time to man the battle stations."

We went into the guest room and ever so quietly opened the window overlooking the back door. A freezing wind drove us to the center of the room, where we patiently waited. At the first bark, we leaped to the window.

"No!", we shouted—though we had to shout in strangled voices, so the neighbors wouldn't hear—and hurled some cans down onto the walk near the back door. "Bang!" "Crash!" How loud they sounded in the early morning stillness! Lupa and Remus looked up at us in amazement; they seemed not to believe what they had just seen and heard. Retreating from the window, we again waited. In a few minutes, after they had convinced themselves that shouts and empty cans could not really have rained down on them, they began once more to bark. We instantly repeated our ludicrous act.

After another three or four days of these dawn engagements, we prevailed. Mornings thereafter found the dogs waiting silently by the back door.

4

Lupa

O nce the dogs had moved indoors during the day, we were in a better position to persuade Lupa that she was safe with us. But her misgivings about people were deeply embedded in her soul. Although we would never know the story of her past life, we felt sure that some cruel, or at least uncaring, people had played a major part in it. We did everything in our power, day after day, to convince her that we were not like the others, that we meant her no harm and indeed that we were very fond of her. But it was clear—for example, from the way she stood (half-crouched, as though ready to run if necessary), from the way she looked at us when we approached her (as if to say, "What are you up to now?")—that we were not making much headway.

As the days passed, I began to feel hurt and offended by Lupa's recalcitrance. I had done everything I could think of to win her affection, and yet she still treated me as a possible threat to her safety. One day early on I wanted to measure the length of her body in order to determine what size mat to buy for her. My motive, as you see, was benevolent, but I made the mistake of approaching her with a ruler in hand. When she saw me, she got up and tried to scramble away. "Stay!" I said, and gently pushed her down. But again she tried to escape. My "Stay!" this time was more severe, and my push had more muscle in it. But she refused to submit to my will and kept creeping away. Finally, humiliated and utterly frustrated, I roared "STAY!" at the frightened animal and shoved her, fairly threw her, violently to the floor. She stayed there trembling, while I measured her body, my own heart pounding, a suffocating remorse already taking me over. According to the philosopher Descartes, God has the power to change things that have happened in the past, even to cancel them altogether. If I were given that kind of power, the first thing I would do is annul that unforgivable outburst of rage against Lupa.

Though it was unforgivable, she nevertheless forgave me. Indeed, we watched with ever increasing delight as she was slowly transformed from the joyless, distrustful wild animal we first knew into our happy and loving companion. The devotion she finally came to feel for us was incomparably moving. The magical symbol of the bond that united her to us was her collar. She wore it, so it seemed, with pride and a certain quiet joy. Whenever we had to remove it, for a bath or for a combing and brushing, she immediately became uneasy and assumed the general appearance, almost, of her old, dispirited self. To restore her confidence, we had only to put her collar back on.

Lupa was cautious and in some ways unsure of herself, but she also had what I call "street smarts"; I mean that she had the will and the cunning to survive even in a hostile world. For example, she was, in her prime, a great hunter. The inexperienced Remus, on spotting a squirrel or a rabbit, would plunge into the underbrush after it, but Lupa, wiser in such matters, would stay out in the clear to pounce on it if it should run from cover. To our dismay, we saw her catch small wild animals and, with terrible shakes of her head, swiftly break their necks. Lupa astonished us a couple of times by actually climbing trees in pursuit of squirrels. They were spruce trees, with innumerable smooth branches sticking straight out from the trunk; Lupa used them as so many rungs of a ladder, and up she went. She never, in our presence, got anywhere near the top of a tree, but on one occasion her back paws were well above my head. Not quite knowing how to descend from that giddy height, she finally allowed herself to sink into my outstretched arms.

Once when Lupa stuck her nose into a muskrat hole in the bank of the stream that runs through the Springdale Golf Course, she received a vicious bite from the animal. When her snout later puffed up, we took her to Jack Blumenthal for a tetanus shot. She happened to be due for another shot as well, so Jack administered that, too. The combination, however, proved too much for Lupa; on our return home, she sagged helplessly to the ground as she tried to get out of the car. A hurried call to Jack sent us racing back to his office: he was waiting with a hypodermic syringe filled with something that counteracted the effect of the two shots. Lupa felt terrible for a day or two, and we were touched by the concern that Remus showed for her. Normally, he would constantly tease her into playing with him, but now he lay quietly by her side and looked on with a worried expression whenever we ministered to her.

Remus not only loved his mother but showed her, most of the time anyway, great deference. When dog biscuits were handed out, he waited until she had received hers, and she was permitted to be first out the door at the start of a walk. During their playful mock fights, Remus, far stronger and more agile than Lupa, never humiliated her, as he easily could have. He had a passion for her urine that amounted to an addiction. Af-

· *Lupa and Remus at play* ·

eorge Pitcher

ter Lupa relieved herself, Remus invariably rushed up to lick the deliciously moistened ground, and then savored the elixir with the same motions of his mouth, the same thoughtful air, that we had observed whenever a friend of ours, a wine connoisseur, ostentatiously assessed the merits of a fine vintage. It's just conceivable that Remus thought his mother's pee contained supernatural powers. Perhaps it did.

Lupa, unlike her son, was a natural stoic. If Remus stepped on a thorn or got icy snow packed between his toes, he crept over to us immediately, pathetically holding up the afflicted paw, begging us to fix it. Lupa would never do that; instead, she would wait where she was, silent and uncomplaining, until we came to her with our magical therapeutic powers. She was in all things more patient than her impetuous son. During one of our many summer visits to the camp of our friends, the Wilmerdings, in Maine, we left the dogs outside the house one day while we went off on a drive that we knew would last three or four hours. On our way back, a mile or so from the camp, we spotted Remus padding along the road toward us; he'd had enough of our absence and was damn well going to find us. Lupa, of course, was quietly waiting for us by the back door.

Whereas Remus assumed that the world was a bright place that was not supposed to contain any pain or hardship in it, Lupa, from bitter experience, knew better. She was resigned to the fact that life was difficult and full of unpleasantness. During another of our holidays in Maine, after the two dogs had returned from a race through the woods, Lupa moved her head every so often in a strange way. At first we could find nothing wrong with her, but when we saw that she couldn't eat or drink, we discovered a small stick shaped at one end like a fishhook embedded firmly, horribly, under her tongue. Despite the pain and enormous discomfort this must have caused her, she never uttered a sound of distress. It was impossible to dislodge the stick, so we drove her to the local vet, a highly competent man with the discouraging name of Dr. Toothaker, who had to give her a general anesthetic to remove the offending object.

Lupa in her prime was aggressive not only toward small wildlife but also toward any female dog who had the audacity to encroach on her territory. Her attacks against invading bitches were mainly for show and never involved actual biting, but they certainly looked ferocious. One expects dogs to defend their turf, but Lupa's territory, as she conceived it, was extensive indeed. It included not only our property and the large farm area next door but also the entire Springdale Golf Course. One day on the course she attacked the unfortunately named Misawee, a perfectly friendly black Lab, and received a bite that permanently scarred her cheek.

She viewed the daily post, too, as it came through the mail slot in the front door, as an invasion of her space. Our postman, if he were to have peered through the slot, would have seen nothing but Lupa's jaws, open, ready to savage the offending bundle of mail. She grabbed it, shook it a few times as though she had murder in her heart, and with a great twist of her neck, hurled it in the air, creating a shower of envelopes and torn paper that fluttered down on the hall steps, over the floor, behind the radiator. Mangled catalogs and toothmarked checks were commonplace in our house.

Since we knew few young children, Lupa was unused to them and they made her nervous. A grandnephew of Ed's, David Freedlander, aged about six, was visiting us once with his family. After starting downstairs to get his breakfast, he came back to his parents' bedroom to announce, "I tried to go down the stairs, but Lupa barked me back up!"

Though Lupa was aggressive toward rabbits, squirrels, intrusive bitches, and the United States mail, she was nevertheless in all other respects a gentle creature. We, in fact, heard her growl exactly once in her life: she was sick, recuperating under a desk in a remote room, when a friend tried to pet her. A menacing rumble, quite soft, emerged from deep within her chest and continued for several seconds. It was a terrifying sound.

We had trained both dogs to obey the usual set of simple commands—"Sit!" "Stay!" etc. When we gave the order "Give me your paw!" we sometimes rewarded them for obeying by giving them a dog biscuit. Lupa was gentle, even ladylike, in the way she gave you her paw—indeed, she often merely waved it just above your hand—and in the way she took the dog biscuit from your hand. Remus, by contrast, thumped his great paw heavily down on your outstretched hand and roughly grabbed the offered biscuit. He would occasionally accompany this performance with an impatient grunt that seemed to say, "Come on, do we really have to go through this nonsense just to get a little dog biscuit?" If we took too long getting ready to walk the dogs, Lupa, in a frenzy of eagerness, protested with her lovely soprano bark, which sometimes trailed off into a high trill, or with an ever so gentle nip on the nose as we bent over to tie a shoelace or put on overshoes.

With strangers she was extremely shy, as she had been with us in the beginning. The arrival of guests sent her scurrying under a piano or to a distant room. Curiosity eventually overcame her worst fears, however, and she soon established herself in the room adjoining the one where we and our guests happened to be, listening without being seen. During dinner parties, we sometimes closed the kitchen door, forgetting that Lupa, in the kitchen, needed to know what was going on in the dining room: then she would nudge the door open just wide enough to stick her head through. After assuring herself with a look around the room that all was in order, she would withdraw to her sentry post in the kitchen.

Lupa, in fact, wanted always to be as close, physically close, to both of us as she possibly could. This posed a problem for her when, as happened almost every day, I was working at my desk on the third floor while Ed was back in his studio on the ground floor. She, in her practical wisdom, solved the problem beautifully by lying on a step in the curve of the front hall stairs, halfway between Ed and me. Being on a curve, the step is wide at one end and narrow at the other; the fit between dog and stair was perfect, for she lay with her ample hind quarters at the wide end and her front paws at the narrow end. This post had the additional advantage of offering her a view, through the small windows that surround the front door, of the brick walk that leads to our house, thus giving her early warning of any invasion from the outside world. She divided her loyalty to us at night, too, for she invariably slept on a landing in the hall outside our rooms, exactly halfway between the two.

Lupa often behaved in ways that we did not understand. For example, whenever Ed or I dialed a number on the living-room telephone, she immediately crept out of the room, as though fleeing some danger. The other telephones in the house lacked this sinister quality. Again, we sometimes found her hiding in her house in the toolshed, unwilling to come out. At our command, "Lupa, come!", she merely put her head down between her paws and looked balefully at us, indicating that sorry, but she had no intention of moving. Had she heard something that we had not, something that frightened her? We never knew. One of the strangest things she did was to bark at anyone leaving the house. She always barked at Ed or me when we went out; you might think she did this by way of protest at our leaving her, but that couldn't be right, for she sometimes barked at guests or the cleaning woman when they left, people she presumably was glad to see go. And for some unknown reason she didn't like people to climb fences; once or twice she made rushes, each happily abortive, at students hopping the fence separating the golf course from the Princeton Inn. A mysterious creature.

You might think Lupa would have been dismissed by the world at large as just another shy, and therefore fairly boring, animal. But no, she had a special quality, no doubt having something to do with her shyness, that drew people to her—was it the vulnerability that one saw in her eyes, her look of having suffered? Certain of our friends earned a special place in our hearts by trying to break down the barrier that she set up around her. Some of them even felt, I think, that if they couldn't get through to her, if she wouldn't accept their blandishments without, as it were, flinching, then there must be something wrong not with her but with themselves.

Kit Bryan was one of these friends. Warm and generous of spirit, she considered it one of her missions in life to help lost souls, people who were unhappy, unsuccessful, unloved. She was thrilled when they were moved to unburden their hearts to her, so that she could help them understand and accept themselves. In a letter she wrote to me not long before her death, she said that this poem by Emily Dickinson expressed her deepest desire in life:

> *If I can stop one Heart from breaking*
> *I shall not live in vain*
> *If I can ease one Life the Aching*
> *Or cool one Pain*
>
> *Or help one fainting Robin*
> *Unto his Nest again*
> *I shall not live in Vain.*

One day when the dogs had been with us for only a year or so, Kit paid us a visit. She had been ill for some time with cancer and, in fact, did not have long to live, but she was still her ebullient self. As we talked, Lupa gazed at us from the darkness under the piano, where she had sought refuge when Kit arrived.

"Look at Lupa," Kit remarked. "I've tried so hard to get close to her, but she still avoids me. I can't bear it."

With that, she walked to the piano, and before our startled eyes stretched herself full out on the rug, and with soft words of endearment, reached out to touch the wet tip of Lupa's nose.

"Oh good," she said when she got up. "She let me touch her. It's a start, a start. But before I die, I've *got* to make friends with her."

And she did.

You would not say of Lupa that she had a sparkling personality; she was not, anyway, forever doing cute or unexpected things that made you laugh. What she had, rather, was character. She was dignified and had great integrity. She did not indulge in wild swings of mood, she did not curry favor with strangers, nor in any way exaggerate her feelings or needs. There was something in the way she moved, in the way she held herself, and above all in the way she looked at you, that spoke of hardships silently endured. She gave you the impression that she had deep, sad thoughts.

The feelings that Ed and I had for Lupa were paradoxical. On the one hand, we loved her and cared for her as parents love and care for their child. But on the other hand, she was also, for us, a mother figure. I'm not quite sure what that means, but I'm certain it's true. Part of what it means, I think, is this: we felt that as long as she was there, we were in some inexplicable way, if not exactly safe from all harm, then at least watched over and generally speaking okay. Because we felt this way about her, the idea of punishing her seemed quite out of the question—unthinkable, really.

One of the problems that had driven me to psychotherapy was a crippling inability to feel and express genuine affection or tenderness. Lupa cured me of that. I was deeply moved by her and never tired of letting her know it. For many months after she came to us, she could not bring herself to lie on her back and resisted my efforts to roll her over into that vulnerable position, but eventually she permitted me to do it. After a while, she not only allowed but positively enjoyed this treatment. She would lie there with her eyes closed, her back legs spread wide, her jaws almost imperceptibly opening and closing in a sign of utter contentment while I rubbed her chest, her tummy, the insides of her thighs, and spoke gently to her. All cares, hers and mine, all doubts about ourselves suddenly gone; just the not quite two of us existing in a space of our own, sharing a world of trust and devotion.

5

Remus

*R*emus in his buoyant puppyhood brought great pleasure into our bachelor lives. I can still see him racing wildly round and round the steep sides of the first tee on the Springdale Golf Course, testing, pushing his new body to its limits. Lupa joins briefly in the fun—or is she only trying to admonish him, in motherly style, to slow down and show some sense?—but she tires soon, leaving Remus to his endless mad circuit. We watch, delighted.

I understood the shining pleasure that parents must feel as their son puts on his first pair of long pants when Remus, one day while still a puppy, nonchalantly lifted his hind leg to pee,

as if he hadn't been squatting to do it all his life. George
Garrett movingly expresses the feeling in this poem:

OR DEATH AND DECEMBER

The Roman Catholic bells of Princeton, New Jersey,
wake me from rousing dreams into a resounding hangover.
Sweet Jesus, my life is hateful to me.
Seven a.m. and time to walk my dog on a leash.

Ice on the sidewalk and in the gutters,
and the wind comes down the one-way street
like a deuce-and-a-half, a six-by, a semi,
huge with a cold load of growls.

There's not one leaf left to bear witness,
with twitch and scuttle, rattle and rasp,
against the blatant roaring of the wrongway wind.
Only my nose running and my face frozen

into a kind of a grin which has nothing to do
with the ice and the wind or death and December,
but joy pure and simple when my black and tan puppy,
for the first time ever, lifts his hind leg to pee.

In the months that followed, Remus was transformed from a cute little puppy into a handsome young dog: he developed a deep chest, a strong neck, long legs, and a lean athletic frame. Unlike Lupa and like a Doberman, he had no undercoat, making him look smaller than his mother, whereas in fact they weighed the same, about forty pounds. On his chest, much narrower than Lupa's, he had a small white cross, a junior version of her resplendent one. He had beautiful, perfectly formed feet; Lupa's were flat, with bony splayed toes, but Remus's were compact, with rounded muscular toes all pointing directly forward. His thighs were as sleek and hard as a horse's.

I had hoped that his ears might eventually stand straight up, like Rin-Tin-Tin's and Lupa's, or that the tips would at any rate fall gently forward, like Lassie's. But no: his ears rose straight up from his head in promising fashion, and then, halfway up, collapsed outward. I don't know that we ever thought of these ears as flawed, but in any case we came to regard them as one of Remus's most endearing features.

His tail was another source of a small early disappointment—to me, at least. I thought it would be nice if his pencillike puppy tail were to grow into a sturdy downward flowing ornament with perhaps a graceful crook near the end. I think I had Lassie once more in mind, though Lupa's tail, too, was rather like what I envisaged. But again no: his tail came straight back at first, continuing the line of his spine, and then arched upward in a triumphant curve. Nature, as usual, proved to be wise, for that tail was just right for Remus; it suited his personality perfectly.

We thought that he must have inherited the shape of his tail from his father, since Lupa's, when it wasn't between her legs, hung straight down. But after Lupa had been with us for some months we noticed that she began carrying her tail aloft, and that it was precisely the shape of Remus's! We were thrilled at this change because it showed that the downward cast must have expressed her insecurity and fearfulness, and that now she was a happy, confident creature, at least with us. Her once dull coat, we were also delighted to see, gradually began to glow with health and, yes, with joy.

Remus matured not only into a strikingly handsome animal but also into one with a bright, happy disposition. On the golf course one day, he leaped up and snatched a handkerchief that was peeking out of Ed's pocket, and pranced proudly off as if carrying the flag of a defeated enemy. After many entreaties of "Thank you, Remus" and an uneasy tug-of-war or two, he finally released his hold on the thing. This thievery on our walks became one of his favorite tricks. We played our part in the act by carrying a rag, carefully placed in an outside pocket so that a corner hung enticingly out. If we should on occasion forget to do this, Remus would at some point put his front paws on Ed's hips or mine and, with head cocked, stare at an empty pocket. He was not satisfied until we provided him with a substitute object—a handkerchief or a glove.

We thought at first that this business with the rag was simply an innocent childhood game. Perhaps in the beginning it was, but it soon developed into something more significant. All through his life, whenever the dogs were left at home for a time, Remus, on our return, immediately and energetically insisted on receiving from us a handkerchief, a glove, a theater program— something, anything. If what he was given was made of paper, he proceeded to chew it to pieces, but if it was cloth or leather, he knew it was to be treated with more respect. We did, however, suffer a few shredded handkerchiefs in the early days before Remus mastered the crucial distinctions.

I think I know why Remus wanted to receive something from us on our return home. He didn't like it when we went away, and imagined that we wouldn't do it if we really cared for him. Certainly when we were about to leave the house without the dogs, he would stare at us with an expression that said, "I don't understand: how can you do this to me?" Therefore, when we came back home—that is, back to him—he needed a sign that, despite everything, we still loved him. So we had to give him a present. My conjecture is borne out by the fact that whenever we had to do something unpleasant to Remus (for example, clip his nails) or do something he, anyway, regarded as unpleasant (for example, examine him for ticks, wash him, or comb and brush him), he would demand, with tail wags and whimpers, a present from us when the dirty work was done. And consider this: if on one of our walks, we happened to meet someone with a dog that we stopped to pet or in some other way made a minor fuss over, Remus would demand his handkerchief as soon as we resumed our walk. He wanted to be assured, I believe, that we hadn't transferred our affections to the other dog. True enough, my hypothesis is gloriously unscientific, but I'll go with it, as they say, until I can think of a better one.

One night after we'd left the dogs in the compound—that is, in the fenced-in backyard—I gave Remus one of my gloves when we got home. He carried it happily about in his usual way while Ed and I stood talking before we entered the house. When we were ready to go in, we saw that he had dropped the glove somewhere. We looked everywhere for it with no luck. Remembering that it was part of the routine that when we wanted him to give back one of our presents, we would hold it while it was still in his mouth and say, "Thank you, Remus," I suddenly got the bright idea of now saying those words to him in a deeply serious tone of voice. He immediately went to a thick bed of pachysandra at the side of the house, picked up the hidden glove, and returned with it. Ever after that, when we wanted him to return a slipper or other nontoy that he'd been carrying around and dropped somewhere—even if an hour or two had passed—we needed only utter the magic words, "Thank you, Remus."

Life with Remus, it need hardly be said, was not always one of pure pleasure. For example, while weeding in the farm one day, I kept a semiwatchful eye on him while he investigated the nearby terrain in his usual way. I looked up at one point, however, and he was gone. He had, in fact, an uncanny knack of quietly leaving the set without anyone's noticing. Often when we were walking with the dogs in broad daylight, watching them more or less carefully, we would suddenly realize that Remus simply wasn't there; he had slipped away on some secret venture. Remus, The Great Disappearer. Sometimes it took us half an hour or more to track him down, but on this occasion in the farm, he came running back in fairly quick response to my calls. But what was this? Yikes! His entire left flank was thickly smeared with a soft tan substance that, when he got within smelling range, overwhelmingly revealed itself to be excrement. Only an animal of elephantine proportions could have produced such an awesome quantity of it. Remus had rolled in it, had ground it deep into his fur, and now came up to me as if he expected me to praise him for finding this wonderful stuff and for having the good sense to adorn himself with it. I did not praise him, however, and neither he nor I enjoyed the cold-water drenching I proceeded to give him with the garden hose. Remus seemed to regard this treatment as highly unjust: one shouldn't be *punished* for such actions—on the contrary!

Remus often vanished from the farm while I was busy with my rows of vegetable plants. So when a young dachshund bitch who was kept tied up in a nearby yard delivered herself of two puppies, we were pretty sure that Remus was the father, since this was not a planned parenthood and the black-and-tan markings of the pups were precisely those of Remus and the mother. But Freddy, an aged beagle belonging to our neighbors, the Pooles, had been seen mounting the inexperienced dachshund, and this convinced them that Freddy had sired the pups. Poor Freddy was soon killed, run over by a car, so the Pooles adopted one of the pups, whom they named Jones. We shall never know with certainty who fathered Jones, but we persist in our view that it was Remus. If you could have miraculously transposed Remus into a dachshund, you would have produced something very like Jones. And Remus had a mysterious power over the younger dog. Whenever they encountered each other on the golf course, even if separated by fifty or a hundred yards,

Remus would stand motionless, staring fixedly at Jones, causing the youngster immediately to lie down, his head on his paws, a picture of total submission. He would not move until Remus, with some look or gesture, released him, at which point Jones would rush over to his idol and lick his face.

Another of Remus's disappearing acts—this time during a walk on the golf course—was frightening. It was a lovely spring morning during that magical period when the leaves of the trees are only half out and the grass has shed its winter drabness in favor of a vibrant green that we have forgotten. Ed, I, and the dogs took our usual morning path along the eighteenth fairway to avoid the golfers starting out on number one. Robins cocked their heads, then pecked furiously at the ground to get at their breakfast of earthworms; I hoped the worms were healthy and nutritious despite the giant machines that regularly sprayed their poison over all the fairways. After passing the Princeton Inn, we lingered for a time near the little lake that intimidates the golfers who must hit over it. We watched a small band of mallards paddling cautiously away from us and admired the daffodils in bloom all round the lake. The resident kingfisher flew over our heads uttering its distinctive rattle.

When we started out again on our walk, Remus had vanished.

"Remus!" we yelled again and again. We blew on the silver

police whistles we carried, no doubt waking up late-sleeping students at the inn.

No response. I began to think that he had found some dreadful object and was eating it. For once my irrational fears were justified, for I found him in a wooded area beyond the inn devouring the entrails of a dead, badly bloated woodchuck. I yanked him away.

"Here he is!" I yelled to Ed, who was searching some distance away, by the eighteenth tee. When he caught up with us, I explained what I had found. "I'm sure the woodchuck died from eating a lot of grass that they've sprayed with their damned poisons. Now Remus is full of the stuff!"

"We've got to get him to vomit it up," said Ed as we raced home. "But what do we give him for that? Milk? Bicarbonate of soda?"

Back home, I frantically rang up Jack Blumenthal's office for instructions. Jack wasn't there, but his assistant told me to force Remus to swallow some vinegar. Ed assumed the dangerous job of holding Remus's jaws apart, while I took the safer assignment of trying to pour the vinegar down his throat. Remus, horrified, wildly protesting, would have none of this; as he thrashed about, the vinegar went into his eyes and ears, down his front, all over our clothes—everywhere but into his stomach. But finally, despite his best efforts, he did swallow a good gulp of the harsh liquid. Out from his heaving belly came a length of the most revolting green sludge I have ever seen. We were immensely relieved, but Remus had lost faith in us entirely. "What," he thought, "have I done to deserve such horrendous punishment?" He crept behind the compost heap, sat down with only his head showing, and gazed at us with a stricken, crushed look that brought tears to our eyes. To make matters worse, I had got the instructions wrong; we should have added egg white to the vinegar to avoid irritating Remus's vocal chords. So when, after a suitable sulk, he barked at us by way of asking for his usual reassuring present, he produced nothing but a tiny hoarse squeak that greatly puzzled him and caused us to hug and pet him.

Remus had everything going for him. He was beautiful and had a winning, positively radiant personality that people recognized at once; on our walks, passersby often smiled down at him with pleasure, and dog-lovers who came to the house immediately wanted to make friends with him. He drew affection and good-will to himself not by rushing up to people with his tail wagging, his body wriggling, as some dogs do; that can be totally endearing, but it was not Remus's way. With guests he didn't know well, he was at first aloof, even a little shy, but after they had been in the house for an hour or so, Remus would come and sit quietly by their chair, looking up at them with an irresistible offer of friendship.

There are certain actors and actresses who, when they come on stage or appear in a film, fill the theater with their presence; our attention is concentrated on them, and their fellow players seem quite ordinary by comparison. When these great actors or actresses leave the scene, there is a noticeable drop in temperature, and we in the audience are eager for their return. They have star quality, and for Ed and me, at least, this is just what Remus had. We found him intrinsically interesting, even when he was doing something quite trivial. For example, when we were expecting people for dinner, we often opened the front door so that he could look through the screen door (or storm door, in winter) to watch out for the arriving guests. He sat erect, ears up, alert, peering out at the driveway with the greatest intensity. Yes, I know there was nothing remarkable about this, but still the sight of him sitting there, motionless, on guard, never failed to move and delight us.

Remus had an uncanny habit, when lying down or sitting in a chair, of assuming positions that were beautiful or in some other way attractive. The call "You must come and see this" was often heard in the house, indicating that one of us had discovered Remus in yet another noteworthy position. It is amazing how he kept finding delightful new ways of arranging the parts of his body. He would lie on his right haunch, his front legs together, stretched out straight in front of him, his head turned slightly to the right with his nose resting on the rug to the right of his front paws, looking like an elongated letter S. Or he would curl himself up in a ball on his favorite chair, his face hidden up to his eyes in the cavity formed by his crossed front legs. Or he might lie in an upholstered armchair, one of his front paws resting on the arm of the chair, the bottom jaw of his upraised head resting against the paw.

And Remus was smart. I said earlier that as a puppy he quickly taught himself, under Lupa's expert tutelage, not to relieve himself in the house. It took him no time at all to learn to sit, lie down, come, stay, speak, heel, and give his paw. We did not often call Remus to heel, and even if several months had passed since we last issued the command, he obeyed at once. Our training in this case, I confess, may have been too harsh, because when he was required to heel, he did so in a crestfallen way, thinking he must have done something wrong; when released from the command, he joyfully demanded a handkerchief, glove, or some other present to be assured that he was still in our good graces.

Over our dining room is a pleasant bedroom where guests stay: the previous owners of the house told us that it has always been called the monk's hole. A door in the dining room gives

· Remus in his favorite chair ·

access to a steep narrow stairway leading up to this room. One night our friend David Pears, who was staying with us, asked to be awakened at an early hour the next morning. At the appointed time, it occurred to us that Remus might be persuaded to make the call, so we opened the door and said, "Go wake David!" Remus immediately raced up the stairs, barked at the motionless form in the bed until he heard a sleepy voice say, "All right, Remus, I'm awake," and then rushed down to us and our plaudits. Thereafter, Remus was our official rouser of guests staying in the monk's hole.

Generally speaking, people are apt to underestimate the intelligence of dogs and other animals. I was certainly amazed by one feat of memory on the part of our two dogs. On our return from a vacation in Maine one summer, we stopped for a few days with a friend in West Stockbridge. The dogs, as always, were with us, and they were much interested in a woodchuck who lived under a tree by the house. A year later, we again visited the same friend after a vacation in Maine; even before the car pulled up to the house, the dogs began barking and whining. When we opened the doors, they flew straight to the woodchuck tree, where they excitedly sought out their old adversary.

Remus occasionally employed his considerable intelligence for purposes of deception. For example, we often gave large biscuits to the two dogs at the same time. Remus invariably wolfed his down, so when he'd finished, Lupa was still working away, in ladylike fashion, on hers. At this point, Remus would sometimes start barking and rushing toward the front door as if someone had rung the doorbell. Lupa, taken in by this ruse, immediately joined in the defense of the house, whereupon Remus quickly returned to devour her abandoned biscuit. And she let him get away with this treachery.

Here's another example. One day on our afternoon walk, Remus and Lupa, catching the scent of deer, disappeared into the woods at the far end of the golf course. For an hour or more we looked for them, calling and whistling, getting ever more worried about them. We found Lupa first, worn out but happily wagging her tail; we were so glad to see her that we hadn't the heart to chastise her. By the time Remus finally appeared, we were frantic. We spoke very sharply to him, though as you might guess, he was soon forgiven. A day or two later, however, the same drama was played out again. As Remus finally emerged from the woods, he caught sight of us on the golf course, maybe fifty yards away from him. He came limping slowly up to us, holding one of his back legs off the ground. Surely he had injured his leg. Had he broken it, or had he perhaps stepped on a nail?

"Oh, Remus!" I said to him, full of compassion and concern. "What's the matter? Let's see your paw."

He rolled on his back, allowing us to examine the injured limb. We found nothing; the leg and paw were in perfect condition. When we had finished our examination, Remus leaped up and began prancing joyfully around—on all four legs— demanding his usual handkerchief present. Ed and I were of course delighted by this bit of trickery; our admiration for his intelligence, if not for his character, soared.

Since Remus deliberately deceived both Lupa and us, it is only fair that he himself should have been duped by another animal. One night as I went down to the farm, accompanied by Remus, to remove slugs from my string bean plants, we discovered an opossum lying inert by the path. He lay on his side, his chest apparently crushed; some vile whitish stuff had run out of his mouth. Obviously dead. Remus barely paused to sniff at the corpse, then moved on. But five minutes later, as we returned to the house, the opossum was gone. He had, of course, only pretended to be dead.

After another "slugfest" (our name for my nightly deslugging visits to the farm) Remus preceded me into the house. When I came in, I was astonished to see an opossum— the same one, for all I knew—lying motionless in the middle of the living-room rug. Remus was resting unconcerned in the next room. He had carried the thing in, believing it to be dead. (Was it supposed to be a gift? Were we meant to think he had killed the animal and, thus, to admire his hunting prowess?) When the opossum saw me, he knew that the jig was up, so he scurried under the low-slung sofa, much to Remus's amazement. With brooms, we tried and failed to shoo the frightened animal gently toward an open outside door. So we left the door open, turned out the lights, and went upstairs. Half an hour later, the creature had escaped into the night.

I myself once unwittingly fooled Remus. Annoyed by the birds that were destroying my young lettuce plants, I set up in the farm a realistic life-size scarecrow, which was dressed in old clothes, including even a hat and running shoes. Remus was visibly startled when he first caught sight of this object; he barked aggressively at it, circling it warily. He was not taken in for long, however; he quickly determined that he was dealing with a mere thing, not a farmyard desperado.

Remus was always anxious to know what was in store for him of an evening, so when Ed and I were getting dressed before dinner, Remus would come up to one of us and look expectantly into his face. This meant, "Okay, what are your plans? What can I look forward to?" If we didn't answer him right away, he would bark, a hint of irritation in his voice, as if to say, "Well?" There were three distinct possibilities: first, we were going out and couldn't take the dogs with us. In this case, we said, dejectedly, "I'm sorry, Remus, but we have to leave you." Then, in a brighter tone, "But we'll be back!" This response, despite the cheeriness at the end, had a crushing effect on Remus; he visibly slumped and, with a hurt expression on his face, went off to lie down. His eyes accused us of betrayal. The second possibility was better: there would be a quiet evening at home. In this case we said to him, "We're staying here with you!" This was more or less what he had expected, so our response brought forth no more than a nod of acknowledgment, as it were. "Okay, right, I was just checking," he seemed to say. The third possibility was the best: we were going to a friend's house for dinner and the dogs had also been invited. "You're coming with us!" we would happily announce, thus producing a frenzy of joyous barking, wiggles, vigorous tail wagging. In a transport of delight, he would pick up a slipper or shoe and race with it from room to room, until, worn out, he would lie down with his head on the slipper or shoe to await the pleasures of the best of all possible evenings.

Remus was gentle and peace-loving by nature, but by no means a coward, standing his ground nobly when challenged by other dogs. He was fascinated by cats but not aggressive toward them; on the contrary, he tried at every opportunity to make friends with them. Unfortunately, the cats we met on our walks either ran away when they saw him, in which case he felt duty bound to chase them, or else they arched their backs in a show of hostility, in which case Remus, once again thwarted in his overtures, shrugged his shoulders, so to speak, and walked on.

Although he sometimes affected to be a free, independent spirit, he was more dependent on us than he was willing to admit. Thus, on our walks, he would often wander far from us, as if indulging in private explorations that had nothing to do with us, but he kept looking back to ensure that we were still there and had not abandoned him. Then, too, when thunder crashed around the house, sending Lupa into the most cavelike space she could find—under a piano, a bed or a desk—Remus, for protection, crept as near to us as he could. Even when there was no danger, he liked to be close to us: for example, on long trips in the car, he spent hours standing on the backseat with his front legs resting on the back of the front seat, between us, often using one of our shoulders as a pillow.

Remus, to our minds, was very nearly the Platonic idea of what a dog should be. Although we were of course highly prejudiced in this assessment, others agreed with it. A student of mine once said, "If you wanted to teach a child what a dog is, you would point to Remus." And one of Ed's students spoke of "Remus, Perfect Pooch." He was not, however, perfect. On more than one occasion when he had been left alone in the house for what he considered to be an intolerable length of time, we returned to find that part of a blanket on one of our beds had been ripped into neat strips by an outraged Remus. These were, I think, the only times we were genuinely angry with him.

6

Ordeal

*D*uring the academic year of 1975–76, I was on sabbatical leave from the university, completing a book about the eighteenth-century philosopher George Berkeley. Just after the first of the new year, my psychiatrist and I agreed that I could stop therapy in the spring, ending nine and a half years of treatment.

"Lupa and Remus—especially Lupa," she told me, "have done more for you than I ever did."

Since the book would be finished by May, and since Ed, too, was free of teaching duties for the spring term, we decided to make an extended trip to Europe—with the dogs, of course. We rented a house from mid-May to mid-July in the tiny village of Mérindol, in Provence, and booked passage aboard the *Queen Elizabeth II.* (We ruled out flying to France on the grounds that Lupa's nerves—and therefore ours, too—would be shattered by a long flight.)

As our departure date approached, we waited until the last possible moment to haul up our suitcases and trunks from the cellar, for we knew that the dogs, at the sight of them, would immediately worry that we might be about to abandon them. On the great day of sailing, after we'd loaded everything into the station wagon of our friend Susan Garrett, who was driving us to the ship in New York, the dogs, who had watched the proceedings with alarm, were immensely relieved when they were permitted into the wagon with us.

As we waited around on the pier, the dogs, now superbly calm amid the turmoil thanks to half a dose of canine tranquilizer, attracted much attention; people came up to pet them, to ask their names, and, without actually saying so, to find out why the hell we were taking two dogs, however nice, to Europe. It was always simply assumed that they were to come with us, despite the possible inconveniences or worse that this plan entailed. We never in fact considered taking any kind of vacation that didn't include the dogs.

After boarding the ship, we installed ourselves in our cabin and then took the dogs up to the kennel, where they were to be housed together in a single cage. We walked them around on the available wooden deck, wondering how ready they would be to relieve themselves on the same material that our floors at home were made of. Remus soon caught on that *this* wooden surface was okay, and proceeded to pee on the simulacrum of a fire hydrant that the Cunard Line had thoughtfully provided. But Lupa fastidiously abstained from answering nature's call. As we left them, Lupa put her nose and paw through the door of the cage, imploring us not to leave her in that totally strange, prisonlike place.

We kept returning to the kennel at every opportunity to reassure the dogs. As we know, memory often distorts things, but as I look back on that trip, it seems to me that we spent nearly half our time up in the kennel walking the dogs on the tiny deck area consigned to them. Almost the only people we met on the ship were other dog and cat owners who happened to be as solicitous about their exiled pets as we were. During the first part of the voyage, Lupa caused us ever increasing anxiety by her inability, or unwillingness, to allow anything to leave her body. It wasn't until the afternoon of the third day at sea that she squatted and let out the contents of her swollen bladder; on and on came the welcome yellow stream. She looked back in astonishment at the pool of warm water that kept spreading over the deck, a body of water that we dubbed Lake Lupa. That night it was martinis and champagne at dinner!

I had private fears, based on absolutely nothing, that the immigration authorities would never let us take our two dogs into France, but when the ship docked at Cherbourg, we were all quickly approved. We had no sooner managed to get the dogs and our large collection of luggage off the ship and onto the pier, than a man from Avis stopped his car near us to ask if we wanted to rent a car.

"No, thank you," I answered cavalierly. "We've rented a car from another agency."

Indeed we had ordered a car that was to be delivered to us on the dock at Cherbourg. But after a thorough search, we found no car, no office of the car agency, and no representative of the agency. While I stood on the pier surrounded by what under those conditions seemed to be a sea of luggage, with two anxious dogs in hand, Ed tried to reach someone from the agency by phone.

"Well, I found out that they never deliver cars at Cherbourg," was his dismal report. "We'd have to go to Paris to pick it up."

But Paris was out of the question. There was no non-hellish way we could get uncounted pieces of luggage and two dogs from this pier in Cherbourg to the office of a car agency in Paris. Even if we did manage to get there, the office, if indeed it existed, would be closed for the night. Besides, we had reservations, beginning that very night, at hotels along the way from Cherbourg to Provence.

By now, the *QEII* was just pulling away from the dock. "Wait! Wait!" I remember thinking. "I want to get on board and go back home!" Before I had time to give way to utter despair, however, the man from Avis, cagily guessing at our stranded condition and noting also, no doubt, my general air of near hysteria, stopped again.

"I've got a Simca that's just been returned," he said. "Would that interest you?"

"Oh yes, it would!" (At last I knew what a knight in shining armor really looks like!)

The Simca suited us—all four of us—perfectly. So away we drove, through country whose beauty was enhanced by our knowledge that we had narrowly escaped, if not a fate worse than death, at any rate an unpleasant fate of one description or another. We agreed that at the first opportunity we would drink a toast to our savior, the Avis agent.

On our trip from Cherbourg to Provence, we had of course to stop at hotels or inns that welcomed travelers with dogs, and whenever possible, we picked places that accepted dogs not only in the rooms but also in the restaurant. The place we'd chosen for the first night, the Château de la Salle near Coutances, was one of these. We decided to give the dogs the big test at once and took them with us to dinner. Since it is unthinkable in America to enter a public eating place with a dog, I couldn't help feeling as we entered the dining room with Lupa and Remus—two mutts, yet—that we were doing something outrageous. I felt sure we would be met with formal contempt from the waiters and, if we were lucky, with only cold stares and nearly silent clucks of disapproval from the other guests. But not at all! There were dogs at several of the tables, and with the exception of the hostess, who could not have been more gracious, our arrival seemed to arouse nothing but general indifference.

But wouldn't this indifference, I thought, turn to disdain if the dogs should behave badly? And how would they behave, I wondered—this stray that we'd taken in off the streets and her untutored son? Trying our best to look dignified and even sophisticated, we sat down uneasily at our assigned table. And the dogs? Without a word from us, they lay down at our feet where they stayed, silent and nearly motionless, as if they had been rigorously trained in restaurant manners. I kept worrying that one of them would do something to spoil it all, but their behavior was impeccable. When we rose from the table at the end of our meal, they got up and followed us quietly out. They had passed the big test beautifully, and we were tremendously proud of them.

The high spot of our journey south was our stay at the Hotel Pic in Valence. While we were enjoying a superb dinner in their restaurant, with Lupa and Remus lying quietly at our feet, hidden by the large white tablecloth, our waiter came up to the table.

"Would your dogs like some food?" he asked.

Yes, they certainly would. A few minutes later, he arrived carrying a great silver tray with two generous servings of beef bourguignon and two bowls of water. It was their first, and last, three-star meal. As we were finishing our dinner, an American couple came in and sat at a nearby table. When we got up to leave and the dogs emerged from their dark recess under the table, the woman was delighted to see them.

"Ooh!" she said. "They have two dogs with them!" We were of course pleased that Lupa and Remus had been so well behaved that she hadn't known they were there.

The next morning when Ed went downstairs to buy a newspaper, he met the American woman in the lobby.

"Où sont les chiens?" she inquired, placing equal emphasis on each of the words. Ed explained that we were Americans, which greatly surprised her, and that the dogs were up in our room. She praised them profusely, endearing herself to Ed.

In fact, during our whole time in France, only one person objected to our bringing the dogs into a restaurant. We had stopped at a country inn, and as we went in to dinner with the dogs, we heard a woman with a New York accent declare in a loud voice: "Oh, why don't they leave them in their room?!" As we had only just passed her table, I stopped to discuss the matter. "Why should we do that?" I angrily asked. The woman was flabbergasted, for of course she had assumed, like our admirer at the Hotel Pic, that anyone bringing their dogs into a restaurant couldn't possibly speak English. She could only manage, weakly, to reply, "Oh ... those rabies." I left this response hanging in the air, unanswered, to vanish of its own silliness. But the woman had succeeded in spoiling the pleasure of the superb dinner we were served, so our spirits were lifted when a young French couple at a nearby table, having no doubt heard the contretemps, lavishly praised Lupa and Remus for their beauty and for their good behavior.

We arrived at our house in the Vaucluse in mid-May. Mérindol is a quiet, undistinguished village on the southern, or unfashionable, side of the Lubéron range, overlooking the Durance Valley. Because it was a center of the heretical Waldensian sect, the old village, which stood just above the modern one, was completely destroyed in 1545 by the villainous Baron of Oppède. After World War II, people from England and elsewhere began buying the ruins of the original houses and restoring them. Our landlords, an English painter and his wife, had converted what remained of three separate cottages into a single enchanting stone house of arches and vaulted ceilings. Part of one wall in the dining room was the bare rock of the Lubéron itself. We knew at once that we were going to love the place— and we did. (The house had one mischievous quirk, however: every time it rained, the roof leaked in a different set of places.)

We began each day by walking the dogs down to the village, across a field where a large flock of sheep grazed, to buy bread for breakfast. We usually bought a baguette, but sometimes, for a special treat, we would get croissants or, when it was available, *fougasse,* a flat, elaborately shaped bread made with olive oil. There were two bakeries in town, both small family businesses. You could sometimes see the bakers, tired from their night's work, their arms covered with flour, relaxing beside their ovens in the room behind the counter. The wonderfully comforting smell of the freshly baked bread made it impossible to think that anything could be seriously wrong in the world.

We did our heavy shopping in Cavaillon, a smallish city eleven miles or so northwest of Mérindol. Noted for its succulent melons, it also had the best wine shop in the province. In the superb cheese store you could find every conceivable sort of goat cheese, irresistibly displayed on huge green leaves in a bright showcase. We bought big bags of dry French dog food in a hardware store there. Lupa and Remus thought it was delicious, proving that they were as fond of French food as we were.

The dogs were a tremendous hit in Cavaillon. One day while Ed was in a store as I waited outside with them, an old man with several days' growth of beard came up to us. After I had assured him that the dogs were *sages* and not *méchants*, he asked what kind of dogs they were. I told him they were mutts, but he scoffed at that. "They're no mutts," he assured me. "That's a breed." (How we wish he were right; for the world, we suppose, would be enriched if there were a breed of Lupas and Remuses.) An old woman once stopped us on the sidewalk to ask if we fed the dogs sugar; it's very good for them, she told us. Then, as we watched in disbelief, she stuck her hand roughly into Remus's mouth to inspect his teeth and gums, which she declared to be in excellent condition. Remus, to his eternal credit, submitted docilely to this extraordinary dental examination. But the greatest tribute came one day as I again stood outside a store with the dogs. Two women of a certain age drove slowly by in their car, smiling and pointing at the dogs. When they came abreast of us, they raised their hands to their mouths and blew kiss after kiss to them.

The dogs thoroughly enjoyed life in Mérindol. Since there was no threat from traffic where we lived, they were allowed to go outside and come in as they pleased. They slept indoors because we had no fenced-in area outside; I loved having the dogs nearby at night, and though he did not quickly admit it, so did Ed. This officially ended the myth that the dogs were "outdoor dogs"; they never slept outdoors again. One of the things Remus liked best about Mérindol was our afternoon walk, for it usually took us up the mountain to a fenced-in field where several goats were kept. Remus was fascinated, almost bewitched, by these animals; he kept staring at them with such focused intensity that he neither heard our commands to come away, nor noticed the increasingly strong tugs we gave to his leash. In the end, we simply had to drag him away by force. We've never quite understood what Remus saw in goats, strikingly handsome though these animals are; he never showed a similar interest in horses, cows, or sheep.

Inevitably, there were a few bad moments for the dogs and hence for us. One hot day in Gigondas after we'd been driving around in our overheated car, Remus nearly had heatstroke. Ed remembered from our dog books that a cold-water dousing was the remedy for this condition; luckily, there was a village fountain close by, and after we nearly drowned a startled Remus with its cool, healing water, he quickly revived. He was certainly back in form by the time we had dinner that night at the Restaurant David in Roussillon. In the middle of our first course, we heard titters from nearby diners. Looking around, we saw Remus halfway across the room, dragging his leash ever so slowly and intently creeping toward a beautiful blond cocker spaniel bitch that we had passed on entering.

Once during a sightseeing trip, we were standing in the town square of a tiny village when a local dog, evidently incensed at our dogs' encroachment on his turf, stormed down from a side street like an enraged missile. He was something out of a Disney cartoon—all flying feet, dust, bared fangs, ferocious growls, coming straight at us. There we were, out in the open, no escape. No sticks or other weapons in sight. Frightened and feeling utterly helpless, we waited for the horrendous encounter. As we tightened our grip on their leashes, Lupa crouched, ready to fight, but Remus, incredibly, remained calm. Motionless, he merely stood and looked at the approaching beast as if to say, "What's got into him?" On he came, this bully, this great village tough. But then, when he was only ten yards away, perhaps bewildered by Remus's saintlike fearlessness, he swerved and ran dejectedly off, almost as if he'd been defeated in battle. Which in a way, of course, he had been.

· Remus and one of his friends ·

* * *

One day late in June we took the dogs with us to Tarascon for a big festival, called the Parade of the Tarasque. The Tarasque was a legendary monster who, in medieval times, had terrorized the town. He used to climb out of the Rhone and gobble up children and animals, and was a menace to anyone attempting to cross the river. Happily, Saint Martha finally subdued the beast by making the sign of the cross at him. Poor shy Lupa was quite nervous enough just because there were so many people milling about the town that day. But when the enormous Tarasque, animated by six or seven pairs of human legs, came down the street and made mock rushes at delightedly screaming children while firecrackers burst, Lupa was terrified.

Then, to our horror, Tartarin, Daudet's famous character, galloped down the street on horseback, firing a rifle repeatedly into the air. We couldn't believe it! Even Remus was now frightened, and Lupa was nearly out of her mind; shaking, she tried to claw her way into the concrete sidewalk. It finally sank into my dim brain that I must take the dogs back to the car, parked half a mile away in a quiet part of town. I can't imagine what people thought when they saw me being dragged along by two apparently demented dogs, with their strangled breathing, their bulging eyes, their nails all but scraping sparks out of the pavement, their bellies half an inch off the ground. I wanted to explain to the startled onlookers that these were really very gentle dogs and that I loved them a lot and treated them very nicely, don't you see, but it's just that they were terrified, poor darlings, by the firecrackers and all. I tried to put on a sort of casual, think-nothing-of-it smile to convey this message, but it's doubtful that anyone noticed. I was, of course, embarrassed at the spectacle we three were creating, but that didn't bother me nearly as much as the agony that Lupa and Remus were going through. I felt stupid and guilty, too, for it was I who had urged that we bring the dogs along to this festival.

In mid-July we left Mérindol and headed back to Cherbourg for the July 22nd sailing of the *QEII.* When, at the appointed hour, we got ourselves and the dogs safely on board, we thought we were virtually home free. Oh sure, the landing at New York might be a bit hectic, but that was the last hurdle; we could handle it, just as we had all the others. We were terribly proud of ourselves: we had actually taken the dogs to Europe and gotten away with it!

The ship pulled out of Cherbourg harbor after dinner, about nine o'clock. The sea was calm, but for some reason, I slept badly. At about four in the morning, fed up with lying awake, I dressed and went to one of the public lounges to write some letters. By the time I got back to our cabin, I was sleepy and looking forward to a couple of hours of blissful unconsciousness. But just as I was about to drop off, the ship's fans that constantly circulated air suddenly stopped, creating an eerie silence. In the distance, I heard, ever so faintly, a siren. And I smelled smoke. I opened the cabin door to find the long corridor outside full of smoke—the corridor that just ten minutes before had been perfectly clear and normal.

"Get up," I yelled to Ed, "and get dressed. Get your life jacket and the lecture notes you've been working on. The ship's on fire."

Up on deck, in the first light of morning, we saw members of the crew in white overalls running about. The ship was dead in the water, its single stack shooting up a thick swirling column of ominous black smoke. Heavy white hoses were everywhere, and strewn over the deck were chunks of black charcoallike stuff. There still had been no announcement over the loudspeaker system, but several other passengers were up on deck, some, like us, with life jackets. We learned from one of the crew members that there had been an explosion and fire in one of the engine rooms, but all was under control. (The rumor circulated later that perhaps the I.R.A. had planted a bomb there while the ship was undergoing repairs a short time before.)

We had been on deck about half an hour when I suddenly

noticed that the port side of the ship's smokestack was blackened and blistered.

"My God," I said to Ed, "the kennel is right there at the base of the smokestack! On the port side! The dogs ..."

I never finished the sentence. I was running. What if flames had swept through the kennel? What if it were full of smoke? My throat instantly went dry with fear. Adrenalin was making a mess of my insides. To get to the kennel you went up to the children's playroom, then through a door marked "Crew Only", along a passageway for a few yards, through another door, and up a stairway. But when I opened the "Crew Only" door, smoke poured out and some crew members came toward me, their faces covered with handkerchiefs.

"Hey, you can't go in there," one of them said to me as if he thought I'd lost my mind.

I may have replied, "I've got to; my dogs are in there," but whether I did or not, that's what I thought. Holding my breath, I got to the second door; to my great relief, the air on the other side of the door, by the stairway, was smokeless. But when I reached the kennel itself, it was locked! Not a sound from inside. Were they all dead, then? There was a second door to the kennel, one that issued onto the deck where the animals could be walked. Out on deck I went, around to that other door, only to find a nine- or ten-foot chain link fence barring the way.

Somehow—my shoes just managing to get mini-toeholds in the fence's openings, my fingers clutching at the wire—I managed to climb over the fence. But the second door, of course, dammit, was also locked. Despair, frustration, rage. I wanted to storm up to the ship's bridge and shout at the captain: "Give me the keys to the goddamn kennel; my dogs are in there; for all you care, the whole place might be full of smoke; and why the hell aren't your kennel people there doing their duty!"

Suddenly, out of nowhere, an image of the first kennel door flashed into my mind: there was a kind of open grill in the bulkhead just underneath it. Maybe I could sniff the kennel air through the grill. So it was over the fence again, back to the first door. I knelt down and fresh air, full of delicious animal odors, was pouring forth from the kennel! I heard a bark, then another. I sat slumped on the deck, weak with relief.

The dogs were safe, all right, but what was to happen next? The explosion and fire had put one of the ship's two engines out of operation, so were we to proceed on our westward voyage at reduced speed with one engine, or were we to return to Southampton for repairs? It was finally decided that the ship should go back to Southampton. Passengers could either wait there for the ship to be repaired, returning to the States whenever it was ready to sail again, or else fly home immediately at the Cunard

Lines' expense. Since there was no telling how long the repairs might take, and since Ed and I had to return home fairly quickly in order to get ready for our fall term classes, we had no choice: we would have to fly home.

The dogs, of course, posed a special problem. In view of England's strict animal quarantine laws, it looked as though they might have to stay on the *QEII* and return to America on it, weeks or months later. But no; arrangements were made that would allow the dogs to fly back with us. They would be put in a van the afternoon before the flight and driven the next day to Heathrow Airport outside London, where they would be loaded into the heated and pressurized baggage compartment of our plane. So their paws would never defile English soil.

We had mixed feelings about this plan: while we were glad that the dogs would be returning with us, we were also haunted by fears that Lupa would suffer horribly. (Remus, young and secure, could endure anything, we thought.) Strangers would take her from the cage she shared with Remus, put her in a separate cage, and load her onto a vehicle she had never seen before. Then she would be driven somewhere, spending endless hours alone in the darkness. How could she know what was happening to her? She would be too frightened to eat or relieve herself. Loaded, then, into the belly of the huge plane, she would hear and feel the terrifying roar of takeoff. (She would die of fright at this, I thought, because back home, she was terrified by the whoosh of the burners of the hot-air balloons that sometimes drifted over the golf course. When she heard that sound, she would instantly head for home, frightened, unstoppable.) Hours later, she would be jolted about on landing, and strangers would again take her cage somewhere. For all she knew, she would never see Ed or me or Remus again: her hardwon world of safety, she would suppose, was lost forever. We couldn't bear to think of her uncomprehending terror.

On the bus that took us from Southampton to Heathrow, I sat glumly next to a window looking out at fields that were brown from a prolonged drought. The scene fit my mood exactly; I was exhausted after a sleepless night, and the immediate future seemed as bleak to me as that parched English countryside.

Our takeoff from Heathrow was delayed for half an hour while we waited for the arrival of the van containing the animals from the *QEII.* Although Ed and I didn't know it at the time, a crisis had nearly erupted over the animals. Another passenger on the ship, traveling with an old and very infirm schnauzer, somehow learned that the van containing the animals was either lost or seriously delayed, and that the airline authorities had decided to ship them on a later flight. The passenger, fearing for the life of his ancient schnauzer, vigorously complained, threatening to inform the rest of us about this plan. "If I tell them," he said to the pilot—and he spoke the truth— "you will have a riot on your hands." The plan was then dropped, and the plane waited for the animal-laden van.

To all outward appearances, the flight home was pleasant enough, but as we got closer and closer to New York, my anxiety about Lupa grew more intense. I could almost feel her suffering, and I dreaded the moment when we would open her cage only to find some half-mad wreck of a dog. The arrival at Kennedy airport was a nightmare. It was one of those insufferably hot, breathless July evenings that turn peaceful citizens into gangsters. With three extra planeloads of *QEII* passengers swelling the already huge crowds of returning tourists, the terminal floor was a chaos of suitcases, packages, cartons. There was a little alcove that said something about quarantine, something about animals; it was empty when we arrived, but that was obviously where the dogs were to be delivered. After what seemed like hours of hunting through the rubblelike mess of luggage, we finally had all our things together and were ready to join one of the mile-long lines of travelers waiting to be cleared by customs. But still no sign of the dogs.

Ed kept outwardly calm through this horrific business in an effort, no doubt, to keep me from erupting into some embarrassing act of panic and outrage. Somebody told us the

shocking news that all the animals from the *QEII* had been pu
outside the terminal, in the street, in the tumult and pollution
of numberless taxis and trucks. Lord, could Lupa survive thi
latest assault on her already battered nerves? And how could we
leave her out there for another hour or more as we waited in
line for customs inspection?

Just as I was on the verge of doing something desperate
one of the other animal owners from the *QEII* pointed out a
customs supervisor who he said would take care of us. I fel
then like the survivor of a shipwreck struggling in the wave
when the rescue boat heaves into sight.

"Okay, you got all the papers for the dogs?" the office
asked. "Yeah, they're in order. Got anything to declare? No? Yo
can go on out then."

Because of our anxiety about Lupa, our expressions o
gratitude to the customs official were, I'm afraid, brief. Out o
the street we found ourselves in an airless, fumy, deafening in
ferno of taxis, taxi dispatchers, harrassed tourists trying to cop
with vast amounts of luggage—and strewn about on the side
walk, thirty or forty animal cages. We found Remus first, sub
dued, happy to see us, basically okay. Then we found Lupa
Crouched in her cage, terror-stricken, she did not recognize u
at first. We coaxed her out and tried to comfort her. She squat

ted, and the pavement was covered with excrement and her bright blood.

Mercifully, the rest of that ghastly night is a blur in my memory. I do recall that in the process of renting a car, we had to reenter the terminal, where Lupa again passed a large amount of bloody excrement. I covered the stuff with newspapers I found in a trash can, unmindful of the stares; I simply could not do more. When we finally reached Princeton, all of us—Ed, I, and the dogs—were in a state of nervous exhaustion.

While relieved to have the dogs back home with us, we were beset with terrible worries about Lupa's health. Remus quickly regained his high spirits, but Lupa was desperately ill with nervous colitis. For days, her body received no nourishment from her food, since her entire digestive system was simply not functioning. Jack Blumenthal tried various remedies, to no effect. Her weight dropped dramatically, and we began to fear for her life.

"I've done everything I can think of," Jack finally told us. "I'm sending you to the animal hospital in Columbus, New Jersey. They've got a bunch of excellent specialists there. Let's see what they can do for Lupa."

We were highly impressed with everything at the hospital in Columbus. The staff consisted of seven or eight specialists—an orthopedist, an ophthalmologist, a cardiologist, etc.—

and there were gleamingly clean rooms fitted out with a
dazzling array of the latest high-tech medical machines. I felt as
if I would want to go there myself for treatment. A young internist examined Lupa, looked over Jack's report, and immediately prescribed some enormous orange pills, a brand-new
medicine. In three days—miracle of miracles!—Lupa was cured.
Thus ended the frightful drama that began with the explosion
in the engine room of the *QEII*.

PART TWO

7

$\mathcal{L}$etting $\mathcal{G}$o—1986

$\mathcal{B}$y 1986, ten years after our trip to France, both Lupa and Remus, like their owners, had become senior citizens: Remus would be twelve in October, and Lupa, by our best estimate, fifteen. Ed and I had retired from the university. Ed was composing, playing the piano, writing scholarly articles, just as he always had. I was writing short stories and the biography of our friend Grace Lambert, and trying to master the subtleties· of the French language. We were living a quiet but contented life in which the dogs played an important part. (A waggish friend quipped that if our work was the warp of our daily existence, the dogs were the woof!) After living together with them for so many years, we—or at least I, at any rate—simply repressed the dreadful knowledge that this happy state of affairs could not go on forever.

One afternoon in April of that year, I returned home to find Lupa in a kind of daze. She came to the front door but didn't exactly greet me; she was staggering around as though drunk. I found that she had vomited in the living room, the dining room, the kitchen. My first thought was that she had eaten some poison, but in a quick frantic search of the house I found no evidence of that. Dr. McMahon, Jack Blumenthal's young colleague, was on duty when I arrived at the vet's; he said that Lupa had suffered a brain seizure, and immediately started intravenous feeding.

Lupa was in dreadful condition at the vet's for the next few days: we thought she recognized us when we came for our daily visits, but that could have been mere wishful thinking. She ate little or nothing, though she would take a few small pieces of chicken from our hands. She could not stand or even sit up, and her eyes were unfocused and moved erratically. She was living in a world of her own. After a few days in which we saw no significant improvement, we were in despair; if her life was going to be like this, then shouldn't it, in fairness to her, be ended?

After she'd been at the vet's for a week, we went out to see her for what we feared might be the last time; we had decided that if Jack told us there was no chance of recovery, we would have to let her go. We went to her cage. She lay there looking forlorn and very ill, though she raised her head to us when she felt our hands on her body, and I thought I detected a faint glimmer of recognition in her eyes.

"She seems to perk up when you come," Jack said after a few minutes. (Lord, what must she be like the rest of the time, we wondered, if this is called "perking up"?) "Carry her out on the lawn and let's see how she acts."

We put her down gently on the fresh new grass where the ground had been warmed by the sun. She was able, but just barely, to hold her head up. We petted her, spoke quietly to her; I kissed the top of her head. Was this, then, to be our farewell to her? The bright calls of a chickadee, full of joy and the promise of new life, only deepened our misery. I mentally begged Lupa to show some sign of improvement, something, anything to keep our hopes alive.

Jack, who had been watching, came out to say, "I think you ought to take her home. Let's try it: she might do better there."

Oh, glory! She was not going to die! Not that day! We blessed Jack in our hearts for this reprieve from her sentence of death.

✻ ✻ ✻

Back home, Lupa lay for hours, unmoving, on a bed we made for her under the pine tree in the backyard. When we lifted her, her legs hung feebly down as though they'd been stuck onto her body with pins. But soon her eyes began to focus and hold steady, and when we approached, her ears would drop down in sweet recognition, as they did before her stroke. She began to eat decent quantities of the boiled chicken we prepared for her. One day we raised her into a sitting position, and her front legs held her up for a time.

Yes, she was getting better, but her hindquarters were still paralyzed. I was bedeviled by the blackest thoughts: she was too old; she couldn't recover completely from such a brain seizure; she would never walk again. I crazily tried to imagine what kind of cart I could construct for her rear end that would allow her to move about. But how could I have so badly underestimated her fierce will to survive? She was in the kitchen one night, and when we came in, she wagged her tail! We rejoiced at the sight because it meant that now some signals were getting through from her brain to the other end of her body. I was as moved by this motion of her tail as I had been by another one, years ago, in the cave under the toolshed.

After four or five days at home, Lupa had not had a bowel movement, so on Jack's instructions, we bought an enema bot-

Lupa with puppies (Remus and Norman)

Young Remus

Lupa in her prime

The dogs at the door

Remus
(photo by Alison Frantz)

Remus and Lupa (photo by Alison Frantz)

Beautiful Lupa

George with Remus

*Ed and the dogs
on the QE II*

*On a stroll through
a village in Provence*

The dogs who came to stay

Remus alone

tle. We put off administering it to her for a day or more, hop-ing that nature would do the job for us. Having decided one af-ternoon that we could wait no longer, we marched determinedly out to the backyard, enema at the ready, only to discover that Lupa had climbed off her mat to relieve herself (magnificently!) and had managed to crawl as far as the toolshed door—on her way, presumably, to the safety of her house in the shed. Ed and I were only half joking when we agreed that Lupa knew the dread enema was imminent, so decided she had better take charge of her own bowels. We were delighted that Lupa had no need of an enema, but positively ecstatic that she had been able to get up by herself and walk a few steps.

Lupa improved rapidly after this. When she had been at the vet's, she no doubt thought she'd been abandoned once again, so, like Milly Theale in *The Wings of the Dove,* she had sim-ply turned her face to the wall. But once back home, reunited with Remus, and looked after by Ed and me, she regained her will to live. Jack Blumenthal knew exactly what he was doing, for he knew the healing power of love. (Jack was to die sud-denly of a stroke a year later, in the summer of 1987. His prac-tice was taken over by a young veterinarian, James Miele, whom we came to trust and admire.)

* * *

After recovering from her brain seizure, though she was basically healthy again, Lupa began to show signs of being what she was, a very old dog. Her hearing and eyesight, for example, became impaired. One night the following fall, while Ed was away lecturing in England, I was invited to dinner at the house of some friends. The dogs were invited as well. We sat outside for drinks, enjoying a cool late September evening, undisturbed by the faint distant thunder. But when we were about to go in for dinner, Lupa had vanished. We called, we whistled, we looked everywhere, even into a neighbor's doghouse. I made heroic but fruitless efforts to appear calm. Lupa must have been frightened by the thunder and crept off somewhere to find shelter. What if she were trying to get back home, I wondered. In that case, she would have to cross several terribly dangerous streets with night fast falling. And she was no longer able to walk long distances. Would she collapse along the road? Lord, where was she?

Between each course of our uneasy dinner, everyone went outside to look for Lupa. We called endlessly, we turned on all the lights in the house so that she might find us. I clung desperately to the thought that Lupa was a survivor. She must turn up, I kept telling myself. After dinner, some three or four hours after she had disappeared, one of my hosts said, "Why don't you drive around in the car and look for her?" I was by this time incapable of thought, so I went along with this suggestion. As I turned a corner not far from the house, the headlights of the car picked up Lupa, lying alertly, patiently, in the middle of the road. She had become disoriented and, in this strange neighborhood, couldn't find her way back to the house. And being partially deaf, she heard none of our calls and whistles. So she lay down in the road, trusting that I would find her. As I rushed out of the car, I expected Lupa to greet me ecstatically—but instead she tried to run away! The headlights had dazzled her, so she couldn't know it was I who was coming toward her. Since she couldn't run fast, I was easily able to catch her. When she felt me and smelled me, she was as happy and relieved to be in my arms as I was to have her there.

About a year later, in the fall of 1987, Lupa suffered a kidney and liver failure that again nearly carried her off. When we got back home after leaving her at the vet's, Remus, instead of leaping at once from the car in his usual way, cringed in a corner of the backseat, refusing to get out. During the week she was away, he ate little and moped joylessly around the house. His spirits revived the moment she came home, and so did Lupa's; she was soon as healthy as a dog her age could be.

By 1988, Lupa was seventeen years old, maybe more. As the year wore on, she sank slowly into infirmity. Her walks got

· *Lupa in old age* ·

shorter and shorter, it became more and more difficult, finally impossible, for her to manage stairs; she grew almost totally deaf, half blind, incontinent. The summer that year in our part of the world, as anyone who was there and lived through it will recall, was horrendously, unrelievedly hot. Although in past years we almost never turned on the air conditioner in Ed's studio, in the summer of 1988 it was going every day, all day, mainly so that Lupa would be comfortable.

Lupa was magnificent during the ordeal of this late part of her life. Several times a day, we carried her out to the backyard so she could relieve herself. Each time, she would fall down at first, but after we supported her in a standing position for a while, she would manage to stand, not too solidly, by herself. She did what she had to do, and then tottered, a few steps at a time, toward the back door. Sometimes she didn't make it, and when we came out to get her, we would find her lying on the grass or hanging half over the low stone wall that separates the lawn from the graveled area, silent, unable to move, patiently waiting to be rescued. Again, she was occasionally able to muster the energy to hobble from the dining room to the front door in defense of the house against intruders. These things symbolized for us the fierce determination with which she battled her infirmities. As Ed put it, she was a model to all of us of how to die.

And clearly, all too clearly, she was dying. Realizing this, I was forever kneeling down to pet her, kiss her, and whisper sweet words to her. I wanted Lupa to have what she had always longed for, the absolute certainty that she was greatly loved. But I did these things also for myself. I was making sure that, however hard her death would be for me, at least I would not be oppressed afterward with the thought that I had neglected to let her know what she meant to me.

We thought that perhaps we were being selfish in allowing Lupa to go on living; mightn't she prefer death to the diminished life she now had? But Dr. Miele, sensing our concern, told us that Lupa would let us know when she had lost interest in living, and so far, we had received no such signal from her. There were still some pleasures left: her appetite was good, and she licked our plates after dinner as avidly as ever. Her expression was alert, and although she was obviously not feeling really well—the arthritis in her hips must have given her a lot of discomfort—she showed no signs of actual pain. She seemed to enjoy being with us, and so we continued to nurse her and to marvel at her quiet courage.

One hot steamy evening in late July, Lupa was lying in Ed's studio while I read the Sunday paper. I was feeling sorry for myself, suffering as I was with a pinched nerve in my neck and a tennis elbow so bad that I couldn't reach my mouth with my right hand. Ed was off at a dinner and a concert afterward that I had to forego. I got up to fix supper for myself to find Lupa looking deep into my eyes with infinite devotion. I was suddenly overcome with a feeling of tenderness for this gallant, beautiful creature. I knelt down by her side and gently stroked her. She raised her head to my hand, eager for its touch, then moved her head gently under my hand, pressing up into it. A great current of love passed between us, as real as a table or a piano. The years of care and worry, the ups and downs of a lifetime together, quietly and gently supported our being together, our knowing each other, understanding one another completely. She might as well have said to me, "I know you love me, and I, for my part, adore you. I trust and love you, whatever happens."

Soon Lupa wasn't able to stand, or even sit up; we could do nothing but wait disconsolately for the end. Remus spent more time than usual lying quietly by her side. When I got up each morning, I found myself half hoping, half dreading, that she had died in her sleep. But in my heart I knew that she would never slip quietly away from us like that, in the middle of the night. It wasn't in her character. But how, I wondered, were we to find the courage to actually give the orders to kill her? Even though we felt sure we would one day have to do that, it nevertheless seemed somehow unthinkable, quite beyond our powers.

One Sunday in mid-August, after we had put Lupa on her bed for the night, she was racked by savage spasms of pain. Her cries were terrifying: stab wounds to the heart. We knew she would never cry out like that unless the pains were unendurable. We called Dr. Miele's answering service, but the operator on watch must have gone to sleep, for there was no answer. How in the world could Lupa, how could we, get through this night? When I petted her, she seemed to calm down a bit, so I made up my mind to spend the night by her side, though I had little hope that this would stop her agony. Just as the whole dreadful situation seemed utterly hopeless, Ed got the brilliant idea of giving Lupa some tranquilizers left over from our trip to Europe twelve years before. They quickly put her into a kind of coma, released, thank God, from pain.

Early the next morning, we took Lupa, still comatose, to Dr. Miele. He checked her over and said what we knew already but dreaded to hear: "It's time to let her go." We nodded our assent, hardly knowing what we were doing. I held her in my arms and Ed petted her as the overdose of anesthesia made its swift deadly way. In a few seconds, her heart stopped beating. Ed, better able to control himself than I, asked the doctor, as we had agreed, to have Lupa cremated. It was unbearably hard for us to remove her collar, the symbol of her trust in us, of her eternal devotion.

Outside in the car, we two sat weeping, plunged into a world of grief. For days after that, tears would strike again, with no warning. Even now, I have to avert my eyes from certain sights—the scratches on the front door made by Lupa as she prepared herself to meet the onslaught of the incoming mail, the smudges she left on the wall next to her bed. And yet I can't think of removing these signs, these visible remnants of her life. I regularly dream of Lupa; so does Ed, and I suppose we always shall. But though she enriches our dream world, her death has left a great empty place in the center of our waking life.

ON THE DEATH OF LUPA

She was here
before we knew it,
silent
under the shed.
Safe for a time,
she must have thought.
Only her pups,
eagerly nursing,
gave the game away.

She was, at first,
a pair of luminescent eyes,
burning bluely
in her cave.
A wild thing,
untouchable.
Her message,
so it seemed,
was "I want only
to be left alone."
Though of course
what she meant
was "Won't you love me?"

How could she know—
how could we—
that when she crept into our lives,
she'd be safe there
forever?

Lupa's ashes, and her collar, lie buried in our backyard under the great pine tree. Over them is a granite stone engraved with the words "Our beloved Lupa."

We shall always be moved by thoughts of Lupa's bravery

and her devotion to us. And these two are connected: for what motivated her to fight against the effects of all her serious illnesses and what kept her struggling so courageously against her last infirmities was not so much our love for her as her boundless love for us. She couldn't bear to leave us. And in a sense that matters, she hasn't: for both Ed and me, she is still, she will always be, a very real presence. She can never leave us.

As I think back over Lupa's life, I realize more and more what a huge debt of gratitude I owe her. The total, unquestioning devotion she lavished on me, as well as on Ed, would be gift enough to be ever thankful for. But by also accepting my love, after being at first so frightened of even the most discreet human overture, she put me, I felt, in a special class of deserving persons. I felt honored. In thus boosting my self-esteem, she satisfied a lifelong, no doubt exaggerated, need of mine.

By the manner of her dying, she brought me for the first time to a mature view of life and death. She taught me what it is to face death with dignity, with patience, with courage. Above all, she taught me how to deal with the death of someone I love. As a child, I had been allowed to avoid all encounters with death. I was never taken to funerals. I was denied, as I explained earlier, even the knowledge of my dog Joe's death. When my mother died, I was an adult but still an innocent child in the matter of facing death. For years I had denied what was obvious to everyone else—that she was dying of cancer. So even at the end, in the hospital she was never to leave, I couldn't allow myself to say good-bye to her. No holding of her hand, no confession of my love and gratitude. Some years later, my father died suddenly and unexpectedly in a faraway place. So again, there was no confrontation with death.

Since I shrouded death in darkness for so long, it was for me mysterious and altogether monstrous. So of course I had grotesque views of it. If those I loved died, that just showed how little they cared for me. It was all their fault. Lupa cured me of these childish, wounding fantasies. She forced me to look death squarely in the face, to acknowledge its reality. She taught me how to be with a person in her dying, how to comfort her. She made vivid for me the plain truths that death is the natural rounding out of a life, that it can even be a desired conclusion. She taught me not to resent a beloved person for dying but rather to cherish her all the more. She taught me how to say farewell. And she taught me, at last, how to grieve.

8

Farewell to Remus

Remus was nearly fourteen years old when Lupa died. They had been inseparable companions and more for his entire life, and he missed her beyond measure. Indeed, he never quite recovered from what was, for him, her sudden, inexplicable disappearance. For weeks after her death, he followed us joylessly from room to room, keeping one or the other of us constantly in sight. Every night as I lay reading in bed before going to sleep, Remus would get down from the chair in which he slept, come to the foot of my bed, and look at me for a few seconds—assuring himself that I was really there and had not surreptitiously deserted him the way Lupa had. And when we had to leave him at home for a time, we would hear him on our return ever so quietly howling to himself. Like us, heartbroken.

It was now evident that Remus was no longer his perpetually youthful self, miraculously defying all laws of aging, but had become what he really was—an old dog. This transformation, accelerated by Lupa's death, no doubt actually began about a year earlier, when he had to be castrated. (I spurn the chilling term "neutered," which horribly suggests that a castrated animal is neither masculine nor feminine.) One virtue of my dark view of life, always expecting the worst, is that once in a while, I will actually spot something objectively dire, as when I noted cracks in a wall that were caused by a rotten beam in the cellar, and a discolored patch in a ceiling that was due to defective plumbing above. So it was I who discovered that one of Remus's testicles was enlarged and hard. We took him out to Dr. Miele, who had just taken over Jack Blumenthal's practice.

"We'll have to remove them," he said. "He's got a tumor. It may be benign, but we can't take any chances."

My heart sank, though I had known all along what he was going to say. This was the first time that we had brought one of the dogs to the new vet for something serious, so he was for us an unknown quantity. And he looked distressingly young and inexperienced to me. My concern for his feelings was no match

· *Remus in a pensive mood* ·

for my worries about Remus's welfare, and I asked him, point-blank, "Have you ever performed this operation before?"

"Oh yes," he answered, with no trace of resentment in his voice, "many times."

"But Remus is so old," I pursued. "Won't it be dangerous to operate on him? I mean, could he stand being knocked out with a general anesthetic?"

"Well, I'm one of only three veterinarians in the county licensed to use a certain anesthetic that's specially designed for older animals. He'll be all right; don't worry." Then, taking his revenge for my callous questioning of his competence, he added, "As a matter of fact, if one of you gentlemen were to have an operation, they would probably use this anesthetic on you."

Remus did survive the operation very well, the tumor was benign, and I became an instant fan of young Dr. Miele.

Not long after Lupa died, Ed and I began planning a trip to France. After the long ordeal of Lupa's decline and death, we felt we needed a real holiday. Somewhere in the south of France, we thought, would be ideal. Remus, of course, must come with us, but in view of his advanced age, flying him to Europe was out of the question, so we had to rely, once again, on the *Queen Elizabeth II.*

We started calling the New York office of the Cunard

Lines around Thanksgiving of 1988 to find out what the sailing dates were going to be. (We were only slightly taken aback
by the telephonic greeting, "Good morning, Cunard Lines.
Welcome aboard!") For weeks they didn't have the 1989 schedule of crossings. Then we got conflicting reports: one agent said
that there might be one eastward crossing that went to
Cherbourg and one westward crossing, a month later, from
Cherbourg. This news came as a shock, for we had been assuming that, as of old, every transatlantic crossing included a stop
at Cherbourg. But another agent had an even more alarming
report—there would be no crossings at all that stopped at the
French port! Just before Christmas, Cunard mailed us the official printed schedule of the 1989 sailings of the *QEII.* To our
somewhat modified delight, it listed just one eastward crossing
(leaving New York on June 28) and just one westward crossing (leaving Southampton on August 5) that stopped at
Cherbourg. This was far from ideal because, in the first place,
July was not the time we wanted to be in Europe, and in the
second place, with only thirty days to spend in France, we had
to scrap any idea of a house in the south, since we didn't want
to spend several of those precious days traveling to and from
that distant part of the country. Still, we might be able to rent
something in the north of France, so we decided to go ahead
and book the two Cherbourg crossings. (We did, in fact, find

a very nice house in the village of Ste. Gemme, fifteen miles west of the center of Paris.)

Imagine our consternation at being told by Cunard, when we attempted to reserve spaces for those crossings, that "we don't necessarily abide by that printed schedule. The word on the Cherbourg crossings is still in the computers—we don't know when we'll know if there will be any stops at Cherbourg." We finally managed to reach a reliable and helpful person at the New York office of Cunard Lines, Mr. Tom Guinan, without whose assistance we would have given up on the company altogether. He made inquiries and, before the end of January, assured us that there really would be those two Cherbourg crossings.

In March we got a startling announcement from Cunard: on the eastward crossing, passengers for Cherbourg would have to pack all their bags, clear out of their staterooms, and get off the ship at Southampton, spend the night in a hotel—at their own expense—and return to the ship the next morning for the Channel crossing. No explanation or apology for this extraordinary scheme was then, or ever, given.

At the same time, we were told that although we had to abandon ship at Southampton, Remus could stay on board that night. (Good!) But—uh-oh—there was an official form granting this permission that had to be signed by someone in a government office in England. Cunard would send us the necessary papers, which we were to fill out and return to them for transmittal to England. Several weeks after we had submitted the forms, we called to find out if Remus's papers had come back from England. We were informed that Cunard had never received them from us. The process, therefore, had to be repeated.

In May, the tickets arrived from Cunard. Our tickets were in order, but what was this? Remus was booked only from New York to Southampton. There was no passage for him from Southampton to Cherbourg, nor back from Cherbourg to New York. I placed a frantic call to the New York office of Cunard.

"Where is the rest of the ticket for our dog?" I asked the agent, a woman with a bright English accent.

"Let me see. Oh yes; we can't possibly issue the remaining part of his ticket until we receive authorization from London for him to stay on board the ship at Southampton."

"But we sent you the necessary papers weeks ago," I helplessly urged.

"You sent them to us?" the voice at the other end of the line sternly asked. "You shouldn't have done that—you should have sent them directly to England."

"But we were told several times by people in your office to send them back to you!"

"I can't imagine why anyone would have told you that,"
she replied.

"Well, what should we do now?" I asked despairingly.

"You might try the British Consulate in New York" was
the helpful response.

Now I knew how Kafka's character K. felt as he sought
entry to the castle.

The British Consulate told us that we could mail Remus's
form to the Ministry of Agriculture, Fisheries and Food in Surrey. "But," the voice added, "it sometimes takes weeks for such
forms to be processed and returned."

And our ship was sailing in little over a month's time! At
this point, Europe seemed like an unattainable objective
shouldn't we just rent a house at the Jersey shore for a
month—if it wasn't already too late?

I was about to give up on the idea of France when Ed
ever resourceful, decided to telephone the Ministry of Agriculture, etc., in Surrey. He was switched from office to office at
the ministry but finally reached Miss H. Brownrigg, whose
name we shall forever honor.

"This is Miss Brownrigg," she said. "How can I help you?"

Ed said later that he instantly felt that he was dealing
with someone who knew what she was talking about and could

solve any problem. He was right. He described our plight to Miss Brownrigg.

"Why, there's no problem here at all," she said. "Your dog doesn't need a form of any kind to stay on board the *QEII* overnight at Southampton. We have a form letter that says precisely this, and I'll mail it right out to you." Which, of course, she did.

Glad tidings! But our faith in the New York office of the Cunard Lines was now irreparably wrecked. Since we couldn't trust them to get Remus's ticket to us by our sailing date, Ed, armed with Miss Brownrigg's letter, went to New York to get it. When he arrived at the office, he was presented with a ticket for Remus from Cherbourg to New York—but not from Southampton to Cherbourg.

"We can't issue that part until we receive authorization from the people in England," he was told yet again.

Ed then produced Brownrigg's letter and demanded to see the trustworthy Mr. Guinan. He read the letter and, after making a few inquiries, handed Ed the missing ticket for Remus.

So we finally had everything we needed to ensure that all three of us could make it to Cherbourg and back aboard the *QEII*. But after our Kafkaesque dealings with the Cunard Lines, we—especially I—couldn't suppress the fear that Remus would simply disappear in Southampton when he was left alone on the ship, lost forever in some impenetrable bureaucratic fog of "Oh, you should have ...", "Well, we don't know anything about that", "It says clearly right here ...", or "Yes, but that's not our fault." (Fortunately, as it happened, Remus did not vanish in Southampton!)

When we boarded the *QEII*, we discovered that certain changes had been made in the kennel since our earlier crossing. The space assigned to dogs and other animals had been moved from the port side to the starboard side and had been reduced in size. In 1976, the ship was still primarily a transatlantic liner, and its large kennel could house some forty animals. But now, in 1989, it had been transformed into a cruise ship, and since people are not likely to take their pets along on cruises, the kennel was smaller, able to accommodate no more than twenty animals.

And there was another change. In 1976, the kennel had been supervised by a pair of young Englishwomen, called kennel maids, who brooked no nonsense. Dogs were let out of their cages only when the owners or one of the maids walked them. All very disciplined and orderly, but they created an atmosphere that was uncomfortably stiff and humorless. Things were quite different under the new kennel master, Romal, an easygoing young man from the Philippines. The first thing he did when he arrived on duty was to release most, and sometimes all, of the dogs from their cages. They frisked and larked about, for all the world like a gang of kids at camp, half in love with their counselor.

Handsome and gentle, Romal had a smile that would melt a heart of ice. He was also a genius at his trade. We found that he was able to size up the character of a dog at once; it was as if he could look into the soul of the animal and read there how it wanted to be treated. Before learning of Romal's virtues and in order to secure preferential treatment for Remus, I pressed a ten-dollar bill into his reluctant hand when we first visited the kennel. But the bribe turned out to be unnecessary, for Romal dealt lovingly and equitably with all the dogs under his care.

On the eastward crossing, the kennel contained five dogs and one cat. There was Rusty, a delightful male of medium size with shaggy hair and a perpetual smile on his face, his tail in constant wagging motion. He reminded us of Hollywood's Benji, utterly irresistible. Toto was a perky, intelligent animal, friendly to everyone but Rusty. I think he may have been jealous of him, sensing that Romal, the other dogs, and all the owners were mad about him. Rusty was quite unmoved by Toto's hostility and seemed not to notice it; saintlike, he was ready to include even him in his general benevolence. This no doubt maddened Toto even further; it took all of Romal's skill to keep him from attacking Rusty.

A tiny Chihuahua spent many hours during the voyage perched in his master's lap, eating tiny bits of chopped meat from the man's hand. Since the family was emigrating to England, the dog would have to go into quarantine for six months before being allowed to enter the country. I felt terribly sad whenever I saw this delicate, coddled creature. Here he was, completely dependent on his master, and headed, without his having the faintest suspicion of it, for six months in prison.

Rex was a miniature strawberry-colored poodle, much adored by the late-sixtyish Italian couple who owned him. They had spent most of their lives in America, but now the husband was in poor health, and they had decided to emigrate back to Italy. In the kennel, they carried Rex endlessly up and down the deck, cooing into his ear, kissing him. Their baby. At first he snarled at the other dogs, and when his owners weren't there, yapped incessantly, ear-piercingly, in his cage. But under Romal's benign influence, he soon became a good citizen.

The weather on the crossing was vile, with never-ending cold winds that were often laced with rain. We owners, bundled to the eyes in our warmest clothes, staggered up and down the short kennel deck, praying that our charges would quickly anwer nature's call. But the dogs, too, had to struggle to keep their balance while the wind wildly swirled their coats. Squinting into the gale and up at us, their companions in misery, they told us what we very well knew, that it was next to impossible to perform the required functions under those conditions. When the battered pairs sought refuge inside the kennel, things were not much better, for the space was stuffy and cramped, and apart from a small bench that was invariably occupied, there was no place to sit down. (When I design my ideal ocean liner, it will include an Astrokennel—a capacious enclosed pleasure palace with AstroTurf, air conditioning, and numerous comfortable chairs in which the owners can sit and read while their pets lie happily at their feet.)

Remus managed to make us feel perpetually guilty during our voyage to Cherbourg. Alone in his cage, he expressed his misery by howling quietly, mournfully. Upon our arrival at the kennel, he would be overcome with relief but couldn't resist letting us know how unhappy our absence had made him. His tail wag, he would utter little high cries and howling barks as we petted him, sounds that we knew well how to interpret. They said, "I'm miserable, stuck here for hours without you, but how happy I am to see you at last!" And when we'd have to put him back in his cage after a visit, he would direct a look of such despair at us that we felt like monsters for closing the door on his

upturned, disconsolate face. Of course this behavior was a form
of emotional blackmail, but it was highly effective, for we spent
far more hours up in that uncomfortable space with him than
we really wanted to.

Remus also worked on us in a different way: abetted by
the bad weather, he refused to urinate or defecate for the first
two days of the voyage. As we walked along a corridor on our
way up to the kennel during this period, Ed pointed out a large
color lithograph by an artist named Passmore. "Yes," I replied
"and I hope Remus will!" When he did, finally, come through
he looked up at us with an expression that said, "Okay, look
what I've done for you. Now the least you can do is stay up
here with me."

After a pleasant month-long stay in our house in Ste. Gemme
we returned to Cherbourg for the return voyage aboard the
QEII. When we handed in our tickets at the Cunard office on
the pier, the young woman who took them noticed something
that we hadn't—on Remus's ticket, he was listed as a "mutt.
Remus is indeed a mutt, but that's for us to say of him, we
thought, not the Cunard Lines. She told us of another ticket
she once saw on which a cat passenger was denominated an
"alley cat."

On this westward crossing, there was, of course, an en

tirely new cast of kennel characters. Well, almost. As we went up for the first time to visit Remus, we met Rex's mistress coming down from the kennel, weeping.

"Never mind, Rex will be okay," I said. "And you'll be seeing him again soon." I put a consoling hand on her shoulder.

"I'm not crying for Rex," she answered, "but for my husband."

"Oh no! What happened to him?" we asked.

"He died!" she wailed, and rushed away.

The poor man had died of a stroke in Italy while they were looking for a place to live out their lives, and now his wife was returning to America with Rex.

The most glamorous tenant of the kennel was a great bloodhound bitch, quite young, who had just come into heat for the first time. Remus, castrated and old, was not interested in her, but Rex was instantly converted into a love machine. He was far too small to attempt coupling with the giant bloodhound, but he tried to mount every reasonably sized dog in sight, whether female or male.

While we were walking Remus during the first day at sea, a young Englishman approached us.

"Pardon me," he said, "but I wonder if you could give me some advice. Do you think I could let my dog out of her cage?"

"Sure you can," we answered. "Why not?"

"Well, the people at Cunard told me that she shouldn't mingle with the other dogs—you know, the dogs that aren't English—because they might have rabies, so she wouldn't be allowed to land in New York or travel to other states."

We were only slightly surprised to learn that the officials of the Cunard Lines in England were as capable as those in New York of handing out masses of misinformation. We explained that the other dogs had all had rabies vaccinations, that if the papers he already had were in order, he would be allowed to take his dog ashore in New York, and finally that in the United States there were no immigration or customs inspectors regulating interstate travel. So Bridie, for that was his dog's name, happily joined the gang. She quickly formed a special passion for Remus, which she expressed often by licking his ear—an endearment that Remus quietly endured.

By far the oldest dog in the kennel, Remus was regarded by everyone—the other dogs, Romal, the other owners—with great respect and affection. For example, virtually every time we came to the kennel, we would find Remus enthroned on the single small bench in the corner, being petted by one person or another. Certainly some of the other dogs would have loved to sit there, but although Remus showed not the slightest aggressiveness by way of defending his comfortable perch, they never thought of challenging his right to occupy it.

Of all Remus's admirers, none were more ardent than a German couple who were traveling with their six-month-old dachshund. We other owners were put to shame by the fact that they seemed to spend the entire day—eight hours or more—in the kennel with their youngster. Even when the weather was foul, they would sit for hours on the outside deck, their backs to the wind, cradling him in their laps. The wife was especially fond of Remus, and although we thought we were being quite virtuous by spending two or three hours with him each day, this was not enough for her. One day when our postlunch nap lasted longer than usual, she looked at us accusingly when we arrived at the kennel and said, "Oh, Remus has been howling all afternoon!" The next morning, as we left the kennel after an hour's visit with Remus, she said, "You're coming back in the afternoon?"—meaning "You damn well better, or risk my displeasure." Another time, as we were leaving the kennel, she demanded of us, "Have you told Remus you're going?"

Because she had Remus's interest at heart, we were not offended but only amused by the German woman's criticism. We even had warm feelings toward the couple because they adopted for the voyage another dachshund who was badly neglected. The owners of this dog came to see him only once during the entire five-day trip. The Germans took him in, however, and he sat happily for hours in the husband's lap while their own dachshund sat in the wife's lap.

By the summer of 1990, Remus was nearly sixteen years old. He had suffered two brain seizures, and though neither was as serious as Lupa's had been, they nevertheless hurried him along the inevitable downward path. They left him with his head cocked to the right—a condition that later improved some-what—and his balance was forever affected, so that he often stumbled as he walked. He couldn't balance on only three legs, so he had to squat to pee, as a puppy does. He found it ex-tremely difficult to maintain the position required for defecat-ing. We watched in tense fascination as he fought with all his might to stop the swaying, fought to keep his body in precar-ious balance, until the unwanted stuff was expelled. Often grav-ity won out over his will, and to keep from falling, he had to run ahead a few steps before continuing the battle. What a re-lief for all of us when the job was finally done!

One afternoon while we were taking Remus for his daily slow outing, we encountered an old man painfully walking to-ward us with the aid of two canes. His face was a mask of mis-ery and gloom. As we met, he scowled at us and said, "I don't approve of keeping animals alive too long." We were outraged at his rudeness, until we realized that the poor man was really talking about himself.

Ed and I didn't consider taking a vacation that summer; indeed, we knew that our next trip would be taken only after Remus was no longer with us. A long ride in the car would have been too hard on him, and besides, we couldn't think of staying anywhere away from home with him because he was by no means perfectly continent. At home we covered all his chairs, sofas, and mats with a layer of rubber and then with old bedsheets. This preserved the furniture, but the washing machine saw heavy service during the last months of his life.

Remus's walks got shorter and shorter; he slept more and more, and ate less and less. His powerful thigh muscles shrank, became flabby; the bones of his skeleton, once covered with firm flesh, showed painfully forth. By late winter, he would eat almost nothing but the white meat of chicken. We would warm bits of the chicken and rice in broth and, with a kind of hopeless, forced gaiety, present it to him as if we thought he couldn't wait to get at it.

"Oh, Remus," we would brightly exclaim, "look at this! Mmm, delicious! Come on, come get your lunch!"

Remus would walk slowly over to his dish and stand looking down at it, while we, holding our breath, pretended not to be watching. He would look over at us, drink some of the broth, perhaps eat a few bits of chicken, and then wander away. He might eat a few more bits of chicken if we insisted, that is to say, if we fed it to him by hand.

It was all too clear that Remus had lost interest in life—Remus, who for us had meant eternal youth and joyfulness! He did nothing but sleep, going outside only to relieve himself and eating only to please us. Dr. Miele, when he examined him, could offer us no false hopes. "Let me know when you're ready," he said. Remus had always detested his visits to the vet's; he trembled uncontrollably in the waiting room, and when he was lifted onto the examining table, panic-stricken, he thrust his head between my arm and my chest as I held him. So we asked Dr. Miele if he would come to our house when the time came. "Of course," he said.

One night at the end of March, Remus was extremely uncomfortable. He wandered about for hours, unable to settle down. We were terrified that, like Lupa, he was soon going to be racked by frightful pain. In the morning, we called Dr. Miele. He would come at noon.

We waited through that terrible morning, stunned with grief and, yes, guilt. We knew we were doing what was best for Remus, and yet there was no escaping the appalling fact that we had asked someone to come into our house and kill our beloved friend.

As he lay in his favorite chair, we petted Remus and spoke gently to him, until tears forced us to flee the room. Suddenly, all too soon, Dr. Miele was there. Remus's blood pressure was so low that the vet had trouble finding a vein to take the lethal injection. But Remus's heart finally stopped beating, and a few seconds later his body gave a convulsive cough that for some reason haunts me to this day. Dr. Miele gently wrapped him in a large blanket and carried him out of our house.

And so, unbelievably, he was gone. Under a stone that reads "Our Blessed Remus 1974–1991" his ashes and his collar lie buried next to those of Lupa.

In the bleak days after Remus's death, I tried to deal with my sorrow by writing about that last visit of Dr. Miele.

The Visitor

You used to sit
at the open door,
ears and eyes at the ready,
alert for signs
of arriving guests.
Why did the sight of you
thrill us so—

for weren't you,
after all,
just sitting there?

When we'd left you
alone in the house
for a time,
you proclaimed
our return
operatically.
The sharp happy barks
rising at the end
to piteous howls
told us
"I'm dying with joy
that you're back,
but—villains!—
don't you know
how I've suffered
all alone
here without you!"

But now you lay in your chair
—oh yes, it's yours,

that chair,
now and forever—
scarcely aware that
this man,
finally,
had come.

(A lifetime ago,
when Lupa led you
and the others,
for the first time ever,
into the bright November day,
you looked at me, then,
with fearless eyes,
your paws on my knee.
"Here I am,"
you all but said,
"Choose me.")

Did you know,
dear Remus,
why he'd come?
But the light was gone

from your eyes.
You couldn't manage to care.

(I see you yet
racing for the woods,
deer-inspired,
your feet disdaining the earth.
Flying!)

Maybe you sensed
somehow
why he'd come?
Your collar hung loose
round your once-strong neck.
You'd no further use for life.
He came to set you free
from what little there was.

Sweet friend:
it's our turn, now,
to wander,
bereft,
in the empty rooms.

9

Caring

Although in the beginning the dogs were my idea, since it was I who was eager to keep them, while Ed only reluctantly went along with the plan, it was not long before both of us were completely devoted to them. To show how much Ed cared for the dogs, let me tell you about something that happened one morning in the fall of 1980. As I was working at my desk on the third floor, I heard a noise in the backyard. Looking out the window, I saw a young man leave our property by the gate next to the toolshed carrying two plastic bags loaded with heavy objects. I thought, "What a strange thing! I'll just go down and see what he's up to."

"What was that man doing out there?" I asked Ed as I

passed his studio on my way out. The studio commands a clear view of the backyard, but Ed, busy with his work, had seen nothing. On I went, and found that the man had stopped a few yards from our vegetable patch. He had put down the bags and, standing on one foot, was tying his shoelaces. I went up to him and asked, "What are you doing?"

"I'm changing my shoes," he replied in a surly manner. I saw no second pair of shoes.

"What were you doing in our backyard?" I continued. I was merely seeking information, trying to understand a puzzling situation.

Like a serpent, the young man uncoiled and delivered a savage blow to my face that sent me reeling, my glasses flying. He struck again, this time on my temple, knocking me to the ground. I remember thinking as I fell, "This is what it's like to die." He jumped on top of me, and was, I suppose, about to do me some great harm, when Ed rushed up.

"Get him off me!" I screamed.

Grabbing him by the shoulders, Ed pulled him off my back. The three of us stood tensely in a little circle, wondering what was going to happen next. Blood was streaming from somewhere on my face. To our immense relief, the young thug decided against trying to deal with the two of us and ran off, never to be seen again. He left behind, besides my destroyed nerves and bloodied face, two shopping bags filled with silver from a neighbor's house. I was bruised body and soul, but I was thankful that since the thief evidently had no weapon, I didn't have to pay for my stupidity with my life.

"But the dogs!" you say. "What has all this to do with the dogs?" The fact that Lupa and Remus took no part in this incident is exactly the point of my story. (Fans of Sherlock Holmes will recall that in "Silver Blaze" one fact of crucial importance in solving the case was that a certain dog did nothing.) When Ed followed me out of the house, he left the dogs inside. And why? Because he didn't want them to get hurt! That shows how he felt about them. I was not, by the way, in the least angry or offended by this, for I would have done exactly the same thing in his place.

Two years later, Ed had a serious operation in Princeton Hospital. As soon as he was able to get up from his bed of pain, he asked me to bring Lupa and Remus around to the street under his room, so that he could see them. He smiled and waved to them while I pointed up toward his room and said, "Look! There's Eddie!" They didn't, I think, actually see him, but at the mention of his name, they wagged their tails and uttered little whimpers, puzzled as they were that the sound of his name was not accompanied by *him*. These long-range visits were, for Ed, high points of his days in the hospital, and when he came home, he was deeply touched at the dogs' joyous welcome. His convalescence, he said, was easier, quicker, and altogether more pleasant because Lupa and Remus were there, sharing it all with him.

Once, while we were walking the dogs on the golf course, I asked Ed, "What if someone kidnapped Remus and Lupa, and demanded as ransom all of your money, your entire fortune. You'd pay it, wouldn't you?" "Of course," he replied simply. On another occasion I said to him, "Suppose someone took a fancy to Remus and Lupa, and offered you ten million dollars for them. Would you think of taking it?" "Certainly not," was his reply. I was not, of course, posing real questions or seeking information: rather, I was expressing my continuing amazement at the fact that we cared so much for these two dogs.

Although Lupa was, as I said, a mother figure to us, we also loved the two dogs in something very like the way parents love their children. I am willing to believe that there is an innate desire in most people to have children, and that since we had none, our paternalistic feelings were transferred to the dogs. So, yes, they were our surrogate children. I say this not to justify our feeling for them, nor on the contrary to admit that it was perverted, misplaced, or in some other way not quite right: I want merely to indicate its quality. Naturally the love of one's dog cannot be as deep and rich as the love of one's child, but it can be in some ways just as intense. For example, our concern for the welfare of Lupa and Remus was, I believe, as strong as a devoted father's for his child's. I was touched to read in the newspaper a few years ago about a man who lost a leg in saving his much loved dog from being killed by a train. I even wrote him a letter of support and encouragement. A utilitarian would doubtless have to say that he acted foolishly, but I, believing that utilitarian considerations are as irrelevant in this case as they would have been if the man's child had been on the tracks, think that his act was entirely praiseworthy.

Part of our feeling for Lupa and Remus certainly derived from this fact that we, like caring parents, took very seriously our responsibility for their welfare; we had, after all, taken them in, had made them dependent on us for everything, for their very lives. Yet another reason we loved them stemmed from the fact that we communicated with them in various ways, subtle and unsubtle. They spoke to us with their actions and with the multitude of sounds they made. They not only told us when it was time for a walk or when they wanted to be fed, but they also let us know if they were frightened, disappointed, happy, contented, or bored. Some of this behavior was of course "natural," in the sense that it would have happened whether we were there or not, but much of it was designed to send a message to us, a message to which we were expected to respond, and to which we did respond.

Here's one example. Once after Lupa had died and Remus was an old dog, April came to stay with us for two months while her mistress, our friend Nini Borgerhoff, underwent a hip operation. April was a delightful, affectionate collie-type dog whom we grew to love. Remus, however, did not love her, wished, in fact, that she were not there, though he politely put up with her. I foolishly allowed April to sleep in my bedroom, and I think Remus sensed, and resented, my evident affection for her. Some months later, Ed and I agreed to take care of April again for a few days. When Nini came to deliver her, unsuspecting Remus made no fuss while we chatted for a while. But when Nini left, leaving April behind, he realized what was afoot. A few minutes later, as I sat alone reading the newspaper at the dining-room table, he came up beside my chair, lifted his leg, and before my unbelieving eyes, emptied his bladder on the rug. I have to confess that even as I scolded him, even as I was cleaning up with the bucket of soapy water, the sponges, and the roll of paper towels, I couldn't help chuckling to myself.

When I thought about this incident later and looked at it from Remus's point of view, I almost wish I hadn't scolded him. Remus had what he considered to be a legitimate gripe and of course had every right to express it. On the one hand he was essentially a gentle creature, so he could not resort to growling at April or biting her. On the other hand, he was not the stoical character that Lupa was; he was not prepared to accept with quiet passivity the slings and arrows of outrageous fortune. He was determined to let us know that he disapproved of this young bitch moving in again on his turf. So he hit on the clever course of ostentatiously peeing on the rug. I had to admit that this expression of his grievance was eloquent, bold, and original.

And just as we received the messages the dogs sent us, so they in turn understood many of our words, actions, and even states of mind. Lupa and Remus are immortalized in *A Bloodsmoor Romance* by our friend Joyce Carol Oates. In the novel, set in the nineteenth century, their "perspicacious master," taking advantage of the contemporary rage for psychic phenomena, presents them to the public as mediums! Lupa and Remus, as far as I know, in fact had no powers to respond to the spirits of the dead, but they certainly understood and reacted to the feelings and moods of the living. I shall always treasure an incident that happened one night while Ed and I were watching television. I was sitting on the floor, with Lupa and Remus lying close by. We saw a documentary about an appealing little English boy who had a congenital heart defect. It showed him at home and in school during the weeks before he was to have

an operation to repair the fault. Finally, his parents took leave
of him, he was wheeled into the operating room, and to my dismay, while they showed close-ups of the boy's exposed heart,
beating, beating, beating, you could hear the surgeons say,
"Uh-oh, that's not so good," "I didn't expect to find that," and
other equally dire things. Well, the boy died, either on the operating table or a few hours later. As the program ended, my
eyes filled with tears. Instantly, both dogs rushed to me, almost
knocking me over backward, and, with plaintive whimpers, fer-
vently licked my eyes, my cheeks, in an effort—which was totally successful—to comfort me. The very same thing happened
again in our house in Provence when the news of Kit Bryan's
death brought a rush of tears to my eyes.

Of all the reasons we had for loving Lupa and Remus,
perhaps the most important was their complete and unwavering
devotion to us. They showed this constantly, in countless
ways—for example, by their dejection when we left them for a
time and by the uninhibited joy with which they celebrated our
return. Whenever we came home after having left them outside,
we would find them standing watch on the low wall outside the
back door, scanning the paths along which they knew we would
return. The first glimpse of us set off a symphony of barks,
howls, whimpers, all accompanied by gyrations, furious tail
wags, great leaps at the high gate separating them from the out-

side world and us. No matter what worries might have been plaguing us, no matter how dreadful a day we may have had, this glad reception never failed to lift our hearts. If they cared that much for us—well, then, our problems couldn't be as bad as we thought.

Yes, we had many reasons for loving Lupa and Remus, but when it comes to love, reasons, as everyone knows, don't count for much. You can list a few if you try, but the list soon gives out, and you are left with what is essentially the inexplicable fact of love itself. So whatever the reasons, beyond all the reasons, we simply loved them with all our hearts; we perhaps even loved them—I'm not ashamed to say it—beyond all reason. And they loved us, too, completely, no holds barred. Such love is perhaps the best thing life has to offer, and we shall always be grateful for having had such an abundance of it to receive and to give for so long a time.

C/820